BEYOND
THE ORANGE
SHIRT STORY

Phyllis Webstad

A collection of stories from family and friends of
Phyllis Webstad before, during, and after their
Residential School experiences.

Phyllis Webstad

Phyllis Webstad (nee Jack) is Northern Secwépemc (Shuswap) from the Stswecem'c Xgat'tem First Nation (Canoe Creek/Dog Creek). She comes from mixed Secwépemc and European ancestry. She was born in Dog Creek and lives in Williams Lake, BC, Canada. Today, Phyllis is married, has one son, a step-son and five grandchildren.

Phyllis earned diplomas in Business Administration from the Nicola Valley Institute of Technology; and in Accounting from Thompson Rivers University (TRU). Phyllis received the 2017 TRU Distinguished Alumni: Community Impact Award for her unprecedented impact on local, provincial, national and international communities through the sharing of her orange shirt story.

Phyllis is the Executive Director of the Orange Shirt Society, and tours the country telling her story and raising awareness about the impacts of the Residential School system. She has now published two books, *"The Orange Shirt Story"* and *"Phyllis's Orange Shirt"* for younger children. These books share her story in her own words. They tell the story of young Phyllis having her orange shirt taken away on her first day of Residential School and never to see it again. A simple orange shirt has become a conversation starter for all aspects of Residential School across Canada and beyond.
For more information on Phyllis Webstad's other books, please refer to the resources section at the back of this book.

I dedicate this book in memory of my beloved grandmother Lena Jack.

Publisher: Teddy Anderson
Design: Eden Sunflower (MWE Staff)
Editor: Kaitlyn Stampflee (MWE Staff)

ISBN: 978-1-989122-75-4
Published in Canada by Medicine Wheel Education.
Printed in PRC.
For more book information go to www.medicinewheel.education

Fraser River cover photo by Angie Mindus
Phyllis Webstad cover photo by Danielle Shack of DS Photography
Back cover family photo by Danielle Shack of DS Photography.
Back cover photo of Gran Lena (bottom right) by Phyllis Webstad.
Dedication page photo of Gran Lena by Phyllis Webstad.

Funded by the Government of Canada — Financé par le gouvernement du Canada

Orange Shirt Society

The Orange Shirt Society is a non-profit organization, based in Williams Lake, B.C., which grew out of the events in 2013, inspired by Chief Fred Robbins' vision for reconciliation. The Orange Shirt Society board is composed of diverse members dedicated to raising awareness of the Residential Schools and supporting the development of Orange Shirt Day.

The Society's purposes:

1.) To support Indian Residential School Reconciliation
2.) To create awareness of the individual, family and community intergenerational impacts of Indian Residential Schools though Orange Shirt Society activities
3.) To create awareness of the concept of "Every Child Matters"

Orange Shirt Day is not just a day on September 30th, it is a year-round educational movement designed to raise awareness of the continuing impacts of Residential School and promote Reconciliation.   By participating and becoming an advocate for this movement, you are changing culture on local, national, and personal levels. By investing your time, energy, and resources into Orange Shirt Day, you are creating a more educated, supportive, and inclusive environment that truly believes "Every Child Matters."

For more information on supporting the Orange Shirt Society and their efforts, including purchasing official Orange Shirt Day T-shirts, please visit www.orangeshirtday.org.

TABLE OF CONTENTS

Territory Acknowledgements
Phyllis Webstad and Medicine Wheel Education acknowledge that this book was created on the traditional territories of the Coast Salish people including the Sc'ianew people, the Lekwungen people, the T'Sou-ke people as well as the traditional territories of the Interior Salish people, the Secwépemc (Shuswap) including the T'exelcemc First Nation(Williams Lake Indian Band) and the Xatśūll First Nation (Soda Creek Indian Band).

What you need to know

The story of Phyllis Webstad and the impact of Orange Shirt Day continues to grow. Thousands of Indigenous and non-Indigenous people now come together, on September 30th and beyond, to honour Residential School Survivors and their families, and to remember those who did not make it. Phyllis Webstad's story inspired a movement. As Phyllis travels and speaks in schools, conferences, organizations, business, etc., there are many questions that extend beyond Phyllis's Residential School experience. It is Phyllis's hope that through this book, Beyond the Orange Shirt Story, these questions may now be answered.

We acknowledge the courage it takes for Survivors and Intergenerational Survivors to share their truths, and in creating this book, we strive to hold a safe space for these Survivors and Intergenerational Survivors to be able to do so.

In order for individuals to truly understand the effects of the Residential School System, one must listen to stories from Survivors and Intergenerational Survivors. Through hearing the personal stories, and learning about the impacts it has had on their personal lives, only then can one begin to comprehend. These truths shed a light on our shared history that may otherwise be unknown. In Phyllis's words,

"The Residential School experience and history is not only Indigenous history, it is Canadian history. It is important for individuals to understand what took place in the Residential School System and the impact thereafter, so that it never happens again. What is forgotten, is often repeated."

The collection of truths from Survivors and Intergenerational Survivors in this book are authentically shared in their own voices. In an effort to maintain authenticity, these stories were only very minimally edited for punctuation and clarity where necessary. The dialogue remains their own. These stories were collected over a four-year period, beginning in 2018. Some stories were voiced in one on one interviews, while others have shared their truths in their own written words. We recognize the difficult nature of these stories and have given storytellers full approval over what is included in their story.

The Survivors and Intergenerational Survivors you will hear from in this book are closely connected to Phyllis Webstad and her Residential School experience. This book does not represent every Survivor and Intergenerational Survivor's experience; all of their personal experiences are different and important.

By listening, learning, and opening your hearts to the stories of Residential School Survivors and Intergenerational Survivors, you acknowledge the true history as you begin to learn from it. No matter how difficult, this is the only way to achieve Indian Residential School Reconciliation. In the words of Phyllis Webstad,

"Reconciliation is only just beginning and everyone has their own understanding of what it means. The truth needs to be told, understood, and accepted before Reconciliation is possible."

As you begin your journey reading these Survivor and Intergenerational Survivor's stories, we ask you to pay close attention to your heart, mind, and feelings. If you feel sad or troubled while reading this book, please take a break and talk to a parent, teacher, or another adult that you trust about what you are feeling.

Canada Based Toll-Free Help Lines

24-hour National Indian Residential School crisis line at
1-866-925-4419

First Nations and Inuit Mental Health and Wellness at
1-855-242-3310

Kids Help Phone at 1-800-668-6868

Suicide Prevention and Support at 1-833-456-4566

9-1-1 Emergency

"In the writing of this book, I've been mindful about the experiences and stories that I've shared. Many horrific things took place during these times, and I've heard stories that I'll keep only for our family and the future generations to read. Awful stuff happened in the past, things no one should ever have to go through. Sometimes the truth is brutal and raw. I've had to really censor what I write and remember the age group that this book is intended for. Everything that is written about in this book is still happening today to many. I continue to pray and hope that we can continue to heal the wounds of the past. It's hard being immersed in this history on a daily basis, and even more so in the writing of this book. Silence kills, so I encourage anyone having difficulty to talk to someone. Call the crisis lines we've listed if needed. Kukstemcw (thank you) for learning what happened to us; for caring and having empathy for our truths."

~ Phyllis Webstad

Phyllis Webstad

Phyllis Webstad (nee Jack), is Northern Secwépemc (Shuswap) from the Stswecem'c Xgat'tem First Nation (Canoe Creek Indian Band). Phyllis comes from mixed Secwépemc and Irish/French heritage. She was born in Dog Creek and now lives in Williams Lake, B.C. She was taken to St. Joseph's Mission Residential School for one year when she was 6-years-old.

Suzanne Edward Jim
(Phyllis Webstad's Great-Grandmother)

Suzanne Edward Jim is Phyllis Webstad's great-grandmother. Born in January 1880, Suzanne was most likely born in Canoe Creek, British Columbia. She grew up in the Traditional Territory of Stswecem'c (Canoe Creek) and Xgat'tem (Dog Creek). Suzanne's youngest child, Lena, was taken from her to attend St. Joseph's Mission Residential School.

Helena (Lena) Jack (nee Billy)
(Phyllis Webstad's Grandmother)

Helena Mary Theresa Billy (also known as Lena) is Phyllis Webstad's grandmother. Lena was born in Dog Creek, B.C. on September 28, 1918. Lena was taken to St. Joseph's Mission Residential School from age 6 to 16. All of Lena's 10 children were also later taken from her to attend.

Rose Wilson nee Jack
(Phyllis Webstad's Mother)

Rose Wilson (nee Jack) is Phyllis Webstad's mother. Rose is from the Stswecem'c/Xgat'tem First Nation (Canoe Creek/Dog Creek). She was taken to St. Joseph's Mission Residential School from age 6 in 1954, to age 16 in 1964.

Theresa Jack
(Phyllis Webstad's Auntie)

Theresa Jack is Phyllis Webstad's aunt. She was born in 1945, the eldest of her mother Lena's 10 children, all of whom were taken from her to attend Residential School. Theresa was taken to St. Joseph's Mission Residential School from age 7 in 1952, to age 16 in 1961.

Hazel Agness Jack
(Phyllis Webstad's Auntie)

Hazel Agness Jack is Phyllis Webstad's aunt. She is from Canoe Creek/Dog Creek Band (Stswecem'c/ Xgat'tem). She chooses to go by her middle name, Agness. Agness was taken to St. Joseph's Mission Residential School in 1956 when she was 6-years-old. Once there, she would soon contract Tuberculosis and remain in hospital for 4 years before returning to The Mission.

Jeremy Boston
(Phyllis Webstad's Son)

Jeremy Boston is Phyllis Webstad's son. Jeremy is Secwépemc, from Dog Creek/Canoe Creek. Jeremy went to the last operating Residential School in Canada for one year in 1996.

Mason and Blake Murphy
(Phyllis Webstad's Grandchildren)

Mason Murphy, age 12, and Blake Murphy, age 17, are Phyllis Webstad's grandchildren. They are Secwépemc, Chilotin, and Chinese, and are from Dog Creek/Canoe Creek. Mason and Blake are the sixth generation of Phyllis Webstad's family to be highlighted in Beyond the Orange Shirt Story.

Phyllis Webstad

I am Phyllis Webstad (nee Jack), I am Northern Secwépemc (Shuswap) from the Stswecem'c Xgat'tem First Nation (Canoe Creek Indian Band). I come from mixed Secwépemc and Irish/French heritage. I was born in Dog Creek and live in Williams Lake, B.C.

Life Before Residential School

"My name is Phyllis Mabel Celestine Jack White." That's what I used to say when I was a child. I tacked "White" onto my last name because I never knew who my father was. I only knew that he was a white man, so this was my only way to have a connection to him. I often felt rejected and treated differently because of the colour of my skin, but never realized until I was much older that my skin was lighter because he was a white man.

I lived with my grandmother on the Dog Creek reserve until I was 10, when my Aunt Agness Jack took me.

I was born in Gran's house on July 13, 1967. My Aunt Theresa tells the story, "We were up Tske7 (the mountain above Dog Creek) picking strawberries, it was July, we were sleeping in the homemade cabins from the sawmill. Your mom woke me up and said she was in labour. I told her to walk, it will help with the labour, and I went back to sleep. Finally, someone woke me up and told me to go get the team. I had to use a flashlight to find them. It was moonlight, so that helped. We put bells on the horses so it wasn't that hard to find them. I had to saddle my horse and ride in front of the team all the way home to Dog Creek. I was the Community Health Nurse, so when we got home, I got busy boiling everything and getting ready. I boiled the scissors and the cloth." Years later, my mom told me that her dad, Francis, sat outside the door awaiting my arrival, insisting that he be the first to hold me. This brought me comfort in my early healing journey when I was feeling that no one loved me.

When I was born, Theresa said she tied the navel and told mom, "It's a boy!" Mom said that she would call me Antoine. It wasn't until Theresa was bathing me that she told mom, "Oh no, it's not a boy, it's a girl!" After that, Theresa used to call me "little Antone," and Mom would get mad at her.

Dog Creek didn't get electricity until 1984. Water was only piped to a tap at the sink, so diapers were washed by hand. Our toilet was an outhouse outside. We had no toilet tissue, just Sears catalogue rubbed together for softness, and Japanese orange wraps at Christmastime.

Our transportation was a team of horses and a wagon. I used to tell my grandfather, Francis, (I called him daddy because everyone did) "Daddy, let's go lop lop." I guess I thought that the clang of the harnesses and the sound of the horses' hooves sounded like 'lop lop'. I have many fond memories and stories about travelling on the wagon.

I remember going to the Fraser River on horseback with my aunt Theresa to fish for sockeye salmon, to a spot that we called "straight down." To get to the river there is a long steep hill, only accessible by horseback. She would tie me behind her on the horse. We would stay there until the wee hours of the morning. I would find a "soft rock" to sleep on. Once, our horse got loose and we ended up walking all the way home. Once, when I was about 15, I counted 25 of us on horseback going fishing straight down. I haven't ridden a horse much since my teenage years, but I have lots of fond memories.

I always knew it was time to go to town when Gran would make a fire to heat up water and wash clothes, and make us take a bath. Baths were in a tub beside the fire. If anyone knocked on the door while we were taking a bath, someone would grab the handle on the tub and swoosh us into the nearest bedroom to finish having our bath.

Most people on the reserve didn't have a car or a truck, so the Dog Creek store owner bought a Bluebird bus, which we called The Stage. I knew it was a Bluebird because I remember reading that over and over on the way to town. I was terrified of motor vehicles. I used to sit behind the bus driver and hang on with both hands on the rail, thinking if I held on tight enough, I could control where the bus went and we wouldn't run off the road.

I never realized why we called that blue bus The Stage, until, when I was writing The Orange Shirt Story, I googled "Dog Creek Stage." Dog Creek is close to the Fraser River and the gold rush trail. To bring supplies and people up and down the gold rush trail in the late 1800's, they used stage coaches. So the people on the reserve likened the blue bus to the stage coaches and shortened it to "The Stage."

Summertime at Gran's was full of activity: planting, harvesting, hunting, and fishing. On a hot summer day it was fun to play in Gran's irrigation water. She would fill a tub (probably the same tub we bathed in) with water and put it at the top of the row. A hose would be in the tub that came from the house tap. To survive, Gran had many gardens. Food was grown and harvested to put in the cellar so we could survive the winter. Fish, deer, and moose meat were dried and stored in the cellar. Back in the day of the ancestors, these cellars were called cache pits.

One of my favourite traditional foods is sxusem, or soapberries. I make juice. From the picking, to the cleaning, to the boiling and then squishing out the juice, and to processing into jars for eventual use; it's hard work. Whenever I make sxusem juice, I realise why Gran had huge hands. It takes a lot of strength to squish all the juice out. I've tried modern juicers but I find that they are just too wasteful. This is a task that many generations of our people have performed. In addition to sxusem, Gran used to tan hides, mostly deer, and make gloves and vests with beading on them. She would make money by selling her beaded gloves, vests, and jackets at the local Dog Creek General Store.

I grew up spending summers by the Fraser River, drying fish with many branches of the family. When I was a kid by the river, we were not allowed to wash our hands or put any parts of our bodies in the water. The thought was that the fish would smell the human and not come close to the bank of the river. I think in those days, they relied on salmon for food, and if they didn't have salmon, they starved. There was no ability to go to the grocery store.

Our relationship to the land is that it is a provider of food and life for everyone, from humans, to fish, to the four-legged. No part of the animal was ever wasted. I've heard people refer to the earth, thus the land, as Mother Earth, and as a 'she', and being a provider of life. Mother Earth is a provider of berries, fish, and wildlife for food and clothing.

My Mom

I never lived with my mother. I remember her coming and going from Gran's house in Dog Creek over the years, but I never went with her. Her story is in this book. I often get asked by students where she was, so I felt it important that her story be told and included.

Mom had me when she was 20. She recently told me how the Indian Agent gave her a letter when I was 3-months-old, telling her she had to leave the reserve to find work because she would not be given welfare to support her and I. The Indian Agent had more authority than the Chief or Matriarchs; you did what they said or you went to jail. Mom was kicked off the refugee camp basically, tossed into a world that didn't accept Indians. Mom said that at Residential School you didn't graduate with a grade 12 like today, that at Residential School, it was age 6-16, and grade 10 was the highest grade. So all she had was a grade 10 education, and she didn't have the self confidence to even get a waitressing job. She, and others from our reserve, ended up going to the USA to work in the canneries, or to the Okanagan to pick fruit.

My Dads

I met the man who accepted me as his daughter when I was 21. I call him Dad John. I say it this way, because for 30 some years, I believed him to be my father. Through a DNA test, I recently discovered that he was not my biological father. I remember the day I found out. It was July 7, 2017, the same day we were evacuated from our home because of wildfires. I remember being at work, checking my email and seeing the test, and at the same time being called that there was fire on the hill. It was a shock and took a while to process.

I found my biological father and met him on December 22, 2018 in Kamloops, B.C. I have met him and all of my biological siblings. Dad Jack is standing behind me in our family picture in this book.

It was a shock for my Dad John. In August 2019, he came to visit from Calgary, AB and took me and my husband Shawn out to dinner at Denny's. He came here to tell me that he still wants to be my father, if I'll still have him. I told him he will always be my father and Grandpa to my son and grandchildren; he has been my Dad since I was 21.

Life During My Residential School Experience

I turned 6 in July 1973, the age for school. I was not unlike other children, I needed something new to wear for my first day of school. Gran and I went to town on The Stage to buy something to go to school in. I chose a bright orange shirt with a shoelace string in front. It was bright and exciting, just like I felt to be going to school for the first time.

If I was told what was to come, I don't recall. Even if I was told, it wouldn't have meant anything, all I knew was that I was now old enough to go to school and that's what I wanted to do.

I remember the morning that my cousin and I could wear our new clothes. We were jumping on the bed, excited to be going to school. We took The Stage to The Mission, about a two hour ride.

I can remember arriving at The Mission. The building was huge, unlike any building I'd ever seen before. I remember lots of crying and the feeling of terror, pee your pants terror! When my clothing, including my new orange shirt, was taken, it didn't matter how much I protested or told them I wanted it back, they didn't listen. This was the beginning of that feeling like I didn't matter. We were made to take a shower, more terror. My baths were by the stove at Gran's; I'd never seen water coming out the walls before. All of us little kids were terrified and crying. We each had our own bed, one in rows of beds. There was a washroom with lots of toilets and sinks.

The Mission was the place where we slept and ate. When I attended in 1973, there were 272 students in total, boys and girls. All of the students were bussed into Williams Lake to attend public school, about 20 minutes away. I was confused, I thought I was already at school. We were put on orange busses to be bussed into town. When my cousin got off to go to school, I got up to go with her, and I was stopped. More terror! I didn't understand any of it. I didn't understand why I wasn't allowed to go with her. I was sent to a different elementary school than my cousin; it was the next stop on the bus. I liked my teacher there, she had crazy red curly hair, she smelled good, and she was kind — I wished she could take me home with her.

My memories of this public school are about the smell of the school, probably the cleaning detergents that were used. Another memory I have of this school is that I didn't want to go outside because of my pants that were red with strawberries on them. I just stood at the door and refused to go outside, because all I could see in the playground were pants like mine, and I didn't want to go out there and be the same as them.

A good memory was my cousin getting on the bus at the end of the day and handing out wild onions that she had picked on the school grounds. On the way back to The Mission, we would sing "We are the missions, mighty mighty missions, everywhere we go-oh, people wanna know-oh, who we are…so we tell them…we are the missions," over and over.

I remember going to church. It was attached to The Mission. This is the only time I remember a uniform, which was a short dress. I felt that it was too small, so I would shuffle along, afraid to move or bend over because I was scared of showing my rear. I hated church because of that.

Girls were seated on the left, and boys on the right.

This was when I realized that I was on my own, that my life was up to me, to never ask for help, that it is up to me to figure it out, that I can depend on no one. (This, I carried with me for the rest of my life…I allowed others to treat me like I didn't matter and I treated myself like I didn't matter. It's still hard to ask for help.)

There was a little Native girl my age who rode the bus with us, but she went home (she lived by The Mission on the same grounds) to her mother and father. I hated her, we all hated her. What was so special about her? She wore "normal" clothes.

Once, one of my aunts came to visit me at the public school. I remember someone came and got me and brought me to her, to the area where we weren't ever allowed to go (now I know it was the administration buildings for the school district). When I saw her I was so happy and I felt hopeful and excited. She must have reassured me because that is a good memory. I didn't cry when she left, so she must have given me a talking to. I think I remember her saying she was working there and she would be watching for me. I remember her kneeling to greet me and talk to me, and I felt important.

I had to really search my memories for any happy or fun times at The Mission. All I remember most is crying, being lonely, and how no one really cared about me or any of us kids. We could cry ourselves to sleep every night and no one would ever come to comfort us.

I remember that a Native woman who worked there was kind to me. She had long hair and a loving face. At the time I didn't know her name, but since then, I've met her again and have learned her name is Gloria Manuel. Gloria still remembers the first time we met when I was just 6-years-old, as she tells me the story:

"I had turned 18 and I was working in the kitchen. We were cleaning up the dining room and getting things ready for the next day. I saw her (Phyllis) walking by, and you couldn't help but notice her. I noticed her face was really red and she wasn't walking fast. I asked her if she was sick and she said, 'Yeah.' She kept walking, because on Friday nights, they watched movies and she was going from the girls' section over to the boys. I went to her supervisor and mentioned that I had seen Phyllis and she was sick, and not too long after that the supervisor took Phyllis out and probably to the infirmary. After that, I would see Phyllis around and I would talk to her, just normal like, 'What's your name?' and she would say her full name, she was such a little cutie. I would see her around and say 'hi,' and she started to come out of her shell a little bit and she would answer."

-Gloria Manuel

Another happy memory is sitting on the floor in line for the canteen, for candy. I'm not sure how that worked, but we got candy occasionally. I don't know how often, but I remember sitting in line waiting and excited to get whatever little candy they gave us.

The food was different. It was not like the food I was used to eating at home with Gran. One memory is of eating eggs. In the dining room, the boys and girls were separated. I remember the noise was loud from all of us cutting up our eggs to eat. I remember eating smelly fish that wasn't salmon, and beans that were shaped funny and had a pasty texture, kidney beans maybe. When I told Gran my story about eating eggs and how noisy it was, her response in disbelief was, "You had eggs?!" Every time I tell this story, it breaks my heart that all the years Gran was at The Mission, she didn't have a single egg to eat.

I don't have a memory of getting my shirt back, or going home when school was out.

Even though The Mission remained open until 1981, I did not go back. A public school opened about a five minute walk from Gran's house, so I went there. It was a one room schoolhouse where kids from the reserve, the store owner's kids, and the ranchers' kids all went. That school is still standing.

My one year experience at The Mission was a walk in the park when compared to the 10 years of my grandmother and mother, aunts and uncles. By the time I attended in 1973/1974, we were allowed to play on the playground with the boys. When they were there, there was a fence separating the boys and girls. Brothers and sisters were not even allowed to speak to each other. If they were found talking to each other, they would be severely punished. The extent of punishment for me was being severely lonely and being made to kneel in a corner until my knees hurt. When my grandmother and her children attended, punishment was severe. At the end of The Orange Shirt Story, I say "Not every child was as lucky as me," this is what I'm referring to by making that statement. The editor wanted me to take it out because he said it was "too dark," but I insisted it be kept in because it is the truth for me, and for my family.

Life After Residential School

When Aunt Agness finished university in Victoria, B.C., she took me from the reserve to live with her. It was a shock to be away from Gran and from the reserve, my first time ever being that far away. We lived with a couple in their home on Government Street. I would wait to cry until I knew no one was home. Then I would cry and cry for Gran, and for home on the reserve. It was during this time that I got my period for the first time. I never wanted to let anyone see my emotion, my feelings, or to ask for help with what was going on with me. I didn't know what a period was, but I wasn't scared either. I just dealt with it on my own. I was too ashamed to tell anybody what I was experiencing and I had already learned that my life was up to me; that my life depended on me.

After leaving Victoria, Agness and I moved back to Williams Lake. The Williams Lake Tribune hired her as a photographer and writer. It wasn't long after that I had my son.

I was 13.8 years old and in grade 8 when my son Jeremy was born. On my 14th birthday, Jeremy was four-months-old. With the help of my Aunt Agness, I was able to raise him and have him know me as his mother. Because my grandmother and mother both attended Residential School for 10 years each, I never knew what a parent was supposed to be like.

But somehow, I instinctively knew what to do and how to care for him. It was like playing dolls; I had a real live doll. I wouldn't wish this experience on anyone. Even though I was in grade 8, I realized years later that the thought of quitting school never once entered my mind. I credit my aunt with that. She raised us both, and giving up was never an option. With her help, I was able to keep my son and have him know me as his mother. I never did have any more children, although I wanted and tried to have more.

I graduated high school at age 17 in Kamloops, B.C. After graduation, my son and I went to live with my son's father in Dog Creek. We moved to Merritt shortly after so I could go to school. I was 21 by now. It didn't work out with my son's father. My son went to live with my aunt once again, while I focused on college.

My son graduated in 2000, and I was on my own for the first time with no spouse and an empty nest. I became an adult adolescent. I jumped out of a perfectly good airplane and went to China. In 2003, I liquidated all my assets, put my stuff in storage, and bought a plane ticket to China to teach English. I only lasted there for 3 months, but when I got back, I ran away to Mexico with a strange man. I'm sure I was a going concern for my family. I had all of my stuff in storage and I lived out of my car for a few months, staying mostly at my aunt's in Dog Creek, as well as by the Fraser River. That fall, I ran out of EI, so I had to find a job and become a responsible adult again.

My Healing Journey

I've often visualised life for my Secwépemc ancestors before the arrival of European settlers, before everything that resulted from their arrival — the smallpox, reserves, and Residential Schools.

My grandmother lived in a pit-house for the first few years of her life. These were houses dug into the ground and covered with earth, and grass was allowed to grow as a roof. There was a hole in the roof to allow for the smoke to escape, and they were cool in the summer, but were mainly winter homes.

All the generations of my family had so much trauma and each generation was never really able to heal from any of it. First there was the smallpox epidemic, then being forced onto reserves, and then being sent to Residential Schools.

I grew up not knowing my own history and wondering why I always felt like I was crazy. I knew something was wrong, but I didn't know what it was called and I didn't know what to do about it. No one ever explained what was happening, or why. I just felt crazy and disconnected from my body. After I had Jeremy, I remember being in the shower and as I was washing my arm I would say, "this is my arm," then I'd wash my leg and I would say, "this is my leg."

I was lost and confused. I didn't have a vocabulary to describe my life and I didn't know where to start to make it better. My focus was on everyone else. I didn't know anything about who I was, what I thought, what I liked or how I felt, and I felt sorry for myself.

At The Mission, and when I lived with Agness, I used to get excited to go to bed because I could go anywhere I wanted. My body would stay in the bed and my spirit could travel anywhere I wanted to go. Sleepwalking and nightmares happened frequently for me. My Aunt Theresa told me, when we would be camped down the river, she would tie her and my feet together so she would be alerted if I tried to get up and sleepwalk. Another word I've since learned to describe this is disassociation.

I was 27 in 1994 when I started my healing journey by admitting myself into the Round Lake Treatment Centre. I learned that focusing on others' lives was not healthy, and that I needed to learn to focus on myself. I learned that I was abandoned, not only physically but emotionally as well, and a lot of the work in the sweat house at Round Lake was to do with this. I didn't grow up with a mother and father, which really affected me in every way.

I never exercised, but at Round Lake, I learned that I needed exercise. I learned that I liked to take walks. Walks helped me physically, they helped me sleep better and feel better emotionally, and I used that time to pray. I called them reality walks. With each step, I would say R-E-A-L-I-T-Y, over and over. I felt like that ostrich with its head stuck in the sand. My head was buried and my butt sticking out was left to deal with the world. I realized that my healing journey depended on me facing the reality of my life. This was the first step for me.

Early in my healing journey, I couldn't say my name without crying. I would say, "My name is Phy..." and I would start crying. Through many years of healing, I have learned that my trauma was an accumulation of all the blows of the past to the generations of my family, plus the accumulation of traumas I had experienced, at the Residential School, and after I left. None of them were ever really dealt with. We were all in survival mode, without really realizing or knowing it.

Two years into my healing journey, my son Jeremy went to a "hockey school" in Duck Lake, Saskatchewan in 1996. We knew people that had attended previously so when my son asked to go, I was okay with it. If it had cost money, I would not have been able to send him. I didn't question it much, I don't remember signing anything. I may have, but as I look back on it, I was still so lost with cotton in my brains and unable to think clearly. Aunt Agness drove him there. She said it was hard leaving him there. When she left, she drove a ways out of sight and pulled over and cried. She said that day she got a feel of what it must have been like for her mother Lena to have her children leave home and be sent to Residential School. Jeremy was only there a short few months and it closed. Again, I didn't question it much as to why it closed. It was in 2007, when the Federal Government was paying Survivors, that we found out it was the last operating Residential School in Canada. Four generations of my family received the Federal Government payment, which was $10,000 for the first year and $3,000 for each additional year.

I've come a long way in my healing journey, starting with Round Lake. First, I needed to be aware, then to accept, then take action – this is known as the three "A's" in my healing program. I've learned about affirmations, which helped me to reprogram my thinking. The two affirmations that I say every night when I get into bed are "I am safe and secure," and "I love myself."

A Year of Positive Change and Awarenesses
In 2004, I took a job for my band as Education Manager and I moved to Dog Creek for a couple of years. The house I lived in was on the same spot as the one in which I was born and grew up. Gran's house had been torn down and another one built in its spot. I felt that my healing journey had come full circle, to be on the land where it all began. While there, I remembered my great-grandmother Suzanne. Sometimes when I would go downstairs, I would smell cigarette smoke about the spot where her room was, and I knew she was visiting. I'd thank her for visiting and watching over me and I'd chat away with her. My only memory of her was that she'd be in bed smoking. I remember how old she looked, and the smell of smoke. Some family members say she smoked like a chimney. I'm told my cousin and I would play a game with her, we would go into her room and say "Mé7e, Mé7e, Mé7e" (yes), and she would playfully try to catch us with the hoop on the end of her cane. I grew up believing in the spirit world. She is forever loved and missed.

Also in 2004, I began to learn my history, starting with the small-pox epidemic of 1862. I grew up and lived beside the Fraser River, yet I didn't know that our Nation was reduced from 30 to 17 bands in a matter of 4 months from November of 1862 to February of 1863. Eight of the 13 extinct bands were in my backyard, and yet it was never talked about. When I learned of it and asked my grandmother if she knew about it, all she said was "yuh," and offered only one story of where her mother told her was a mass burial. That was it, never to be discussed again. It's my personal commitment to remember those people, to remember where I came from, and to teach my child and my grandchildren about it. I realized that some-one in every family survived the smallpox for us all to be here. What I've learned is that my family was away from the Fraser River when the small-pox hit. My great-grandmother Suzanne's family were in their pit houses at Big Lake, also known as Gustafson Lake.

My first grandson, Blake, was born on August 11, 2004. I was in awe! I wanted to be the best grandmother possible! He taught me so much. When I would look at him and feel how much love I felt for him, I realised that of course Gran loved me. As I looked at him I would think, "How can a grandmother not love her grandchildren," and I realized that my feelings of not being loved were all wrong. Of course she loved me!

This is something I wrote to Blake on a lunch break from work in Dog Creek:

"What a blessing it was today to bring you out for a walk. I took you out on my lunch hour, I hated to rush you, and I ended up being 15 minutes late for work. It is thawing in Dog Creek, run off, ice and muck and mud – but you loved it all!

We couldn't find your other rubber boot, so I just put on your boots your grandpa got you for Christmas. I always learn so much from you. I get so busy with life that I forget about the wonders of life. Like today, you were so in awe with the streams of runoff, crouched down, listening, looking up and down the little stream of water running, looking at the bubbles, stamping it all with one foot on occasion. Then...the mud! You just loved the mud, you'd jump up and down in it, and just look down at your feet for a long time, watching your feet in the mud. I just stood on the road, letting you, watching you doing these things for the first time – it's such a joy for me. I never did these things with your father, not that I remember anyway.

Splashing in the puddles, you'd make a big splash and I'd clap. I just have so much love for you, my grandson. Watching you, I was thinking about how I must have done those same things as a child.

When we got back to the house, your pants and shoes were wet and muddy and your socks were soaking wet also. After I took your pants, shoes, and socks off, you crouched down and said "cold." I sent you into the room to your Grandma Elsie so she could put some clothes on you. I then had to rush out the door and scurry back to work."

My son now has five children, and I have five beautiful grandchildren! I am so blessed with them all! I am so proud of my son, he works so hard to support his wife and children. My daughter-in-law stays home and takes care of the children. I learned just how strong she is when she landed in the hospital for a week a couple of years ago, and the grandmas stepped in (her mom and I) to look after the kids and household until she returned. It was a very long week for someone not used to looking after small children. She just makes it seem so easy.

As an adult, I had stopped spending summers by the Fraser River catching and drying fish. When my cousin and I became grandmothers, we discussed wanting the same memories for our grandchildren that we had. So we decided to start our annual family fish camp in August. I tell my grandchildren about what I was taught and what it was like for me by the river as a young girl.

I never connected my history or my healing journey to my Residential School experience until 2013 when the TRC (Truth and Reconciliation Commission) came to Williams Lake. It was then that I really began to understand. This is a quote from that time, "I finally get it, that the feeling of worthlessness and insignificance, ingrained in me from my first day at The Mission, affected the way I lived my life for many years. Even now, when I know nothing could be further than the truth, I still sometimes feel that I don't matter. Even with all the work I've done!"

I get given messages in random ways, such as recently on my drive to the office. In my journal I wrote:

"Today, driving to work, I saw three little girls lined up as the bus approached with its red lights flashing. As I passed by them, the words 'it's okay' were spoken to me and I felt it in my soul. The memory triggered was that of getting on the bus to go to Residential School and public school, and all that followed. Such a tiny quick moment but it was a healing moment nonetheless. It brought a tear to my eye."

Final Thoughts

Students wanting to learn more have been my motivation for writing books about my experience at The Mission. I was being asked to go into elementary schools and tell my orange shirt story, but it was hard to stand in front of children and tell them what happened; I thought if I had a book with pictures, I could explain it better. My motivation for this book is the same. When presenting and talking with middle and high school students, they want to learn more about what happened and what it was like. I was only at The Mission for one year, and being only 6-years-old, my memories are few. I thought, if I can get others in my family, my teacher, and a woman that was nice to me to write about their experiences in relation to my Orange Shirt Story, to myself, and to The Mission, then the older students can learn more about what happened and what it was like.

From the very beginning, Orange Shirt Day has been divinely guided; I think this also pertains to my life as well. I believe that the ancestors are with me, giving me strength and guiding me through life.

My story is not unique. At least 150,000 children attended Residential Schools across Canada. Each of them has a truth, a story to tell. Their families have a story to tell. I've found that memories may differ among those that encountered the same situation or event, and that's okay; we are all entitled to our own truth. I encourage you to seek out Survivors and their families to hear their truths.

The Residential School story is complicated for families because the kids who went there made the most of it. This book tells the story of many in my family. Even with all the bad things that happened, when we are together talking about Residential School, humour finds its way into our conversations. Humour can be healing.

It is scary, and sometimes retraumatizing, putting myself and my family out there. It is my hope that our truths will help others to understand that this is not only Indigenous history, this is Canadian history. There is no longer any excuse for Canadians being unaware of the Residential School history and the intergenerational impacts that are still here today. So this is my challenge to everyone reading this book: please share what you've learned with anyone who still doesn't know.

It's hard being immersed in this history on a daily basis, including the writing of this book. I was recently asked how I do it, what do I do to take care of myself? Do I ever feel like giving up? My answer was yes, at times I do feel like just walking away, but it's a good thing that feelings aren't facts. I can feel this way, but I don't have to act on it. I will continue on my healing journey path of self-care, take each day as it comes, and do my best each day. This is all I can do. Life can be understood backwards but must be lived forwards — I can talk about the past in order to teach and help myself and others grow, but I cannot stay there, I must call my spirit back to today and look forward to tomorrow and what it will bring.

My healing journey will continue until I leave this earth. If I don't keep up with my program, with therapy, and a healthy lifestyle, I can quickly find myself under a black cloud of negative thinking. At times, it is necessary to seek professional help with my mental wellness; I encourage everyone to do the same when it is needed.

This book and the stories in it are not intended to blame anyone for anything or to shame anyone. I believe that we are all doing the best we can with what we have and what we know. When we know better, we will do better.

I want people to know that Residential Schools were real, they happened. And the long-lasting intergenerational impacts are real and happening still today, in 2021. My great-grandmother Suzanne was the first generation in my family to have a child that attended Residential School — my Gran Lena; she is a Survivor. Lena's 10 children attended, including my mother Rose, and my aunties Agness and Theresa; therefore, my mother and aunties are Survivors and Intergenerational Survivors. I attended for one year; therefore, I'm a Survivor and Intergenerational Survivor. My son Jeremy also attended Residential School, he is a Survivor and Intergenerational Survivor. Jeremy's five children, including my grandsons Blake and Mason are Intergenerational Survivors. That is six generations of my family that have been directly impacted by the Residential School System. These institutions were real, they happened.

In the writing of this book, I've been mindful about the experiences and stories that I have chosen to share. Many horrific things took place during these times, and I've heard stories that I'll keep only for our family and the future generations to read. Sometimes the truth is brutal and raw. I continue to pray and hope that we can continue to heal the wounds of the past.

> Kukstemcw (thank you) to my family for being there and supporting me. I thank you, the reader, for learning what happened to us; for caring and having empathy for our truths.
> ~ Phyllis Webstad

Suzanne Edward Jim (Phyllis Webstad's Great-Grandmother)

Written by Phyllis Webstad with the help of her aunties Theresa Jack and Agness Jack, as well as her mother Rose Wilson.

Suzanne Edward Jim is my (Phyllis Webstad)'s great-grandmother. Born in January 1880 to Chief Johnny Noriaskret aka Copper Johnny, her father, and Aspikenac aka Madeleine, her mother. Suzanne was most likely born in Canoe Creek, British Columbia. She grew up in the Traditional Territory of Stswecem'c (Canoe Creek) and Xgat'tem (Dog Creek).

Great-grandmother Suzanne grew up living in a traditional Secwépemc, or Shuswap pit home at Big Lake, or now known as Gustafson Lake. Her first language was Secwepemctsín. She could understand and speak English as well.

Suzanne was married twice. Her first marriage was to Edward Skouetalist in about 1903. They lived right next to the graveyard in Dog Creek, which she blamed for them losing the majority of their children. Their first nine children did not survive; she felt that God was taking them away. A decision was made to move further away from the graveyard, only then did the children survive, they were Joe, Alfie, and Felecia.

Her second marriage was in 1939 to George James Stanislas Jim; they never had any children together. Great-grandmother Suzanne became known as Suzanne Edward Jim, adopting both names from her husbands.

Suzanne's youngest child was my grandmother, Helena, or Lena, named after Suzanne's aunt. Although Lena's biological father was Moses Billy, she called George her dad. My aunt Agness remembers fondly that, "My Granny Suzanne loved her baby Lena so much. When Mom [Lena] would visit Suzanne later in life, Suzanne would run around the wagon and be so happy to see her Lena. They would hold

Photo of Great-grandmother Suzanne Edward Jim, Photographer Unknown.

each other and hug, only then would kyé7e (grandmother) Suzanne say hello to the rest of us."

Great-grandmother Suzanne never drank alcohol. She had a sense of humour and was easy-going. She loved to dance, sing, listen to music on the radio, and bake bread. When she would dance, everyone would disappear because they didn't want to be made to dance with her. She was a hard worker and she loved to tell funny stories, too! She made the best bread. Her children used to hang around outside and wait for the bread to be ready. She was an amazing cook and she always cooked potatoes. She loved porcupine and rabbit.

She had a lot of gardens, big long gardens, two in Dog Creek and two down by the Fraser River, even a garden up the mountain by Dog Creek that we call Tske7. She was really strong and active. In her gardens, she grew watermelon, cucumbers, potatoes, corn, carrots, and turnips to name a few. In the fall, when the digging for harvest was done, she would give out veggies by the sack. My aunt Theresa wondered how she could do that when some people treated her bad. She would share her harvest with others in the community, even those that weren't nice to her. That was the Secwépemc way though — caring & sharing. She was always helpful and thoughtful to everyone; she had a heart for everybody. Even with her enemies, she wouldn't hold anything against them. When people killed some of her chickens, she didn't talk bad about those people.

Suzanne was a devout Catholic. I believe her mother, Madeleine, was also Catholic, and I'm not sure beyond that. Great-grandmother Suzanne attended church and knew the prayers and hymns in Shuswap. In church, she often led the prayers taught to her by Father Thomas. My Aunt Theresa recalls that, "Father Thomas learned our language and taught the older generation the prayers and hymns. My Granny Suzanne really believed in the Catholic faith, her and my mom [Lena]. I believe that's why they both lived so long."

Suzanne did not attend Residential School and she did not know how to read or write. Aunt Theresa says that Suzanne was the first mother in our family who watched her daughter, Lena, leave to attend a Residential School. When Lena was old enough, she attended Residential School. My Great-grandmother Suzanne gave Lena two sweaters so that she would be warm in the winter. The Sister at the school took one away and gave it to another girl. Out of all of Suzanne's children, only Lena went to Residential School. Suzanne would visit Lena at the Residential School by horseback.

Aunt Theresa tells a story about how Suzanne didn't know when her own birthday was, so Theresa told her January 1st. So, every January 1st, Suzanne would give Theresa money to buy a box of Japanese oranges to celebrate her birthday.

In 1972, Suzanne broke her hip. She was quarantined while in the Williams Lake hospital because of a sickness going on. No one was allowed to see her or visit. The hospital was going to allow family to see her though, because they said she was almost passing. But before anyone could go and see her, she had already passed. My Great-grandmother Suzanne died alone in the Williams Lake hospital on December 25, 1972. She is buried in the Dog Creek cemetery.

I just recently found baptismal information for Suzanne from the Royal BC Museum that states she was born in January 1880, which would mean she was 92 when she passed in 1972. This is the only information I've been able to find on her birth. I believe that family lore will continue that she lived to be 110.

"In the fall, when the digging for harvest was done, she would give out veggies by the sack... She would share her harvest with others in the community, even those that weren't nice to her. That was the Secwépemc way though — caring & sharing."

Helena (Lena) Jack (nee Billy) (Phyllis Webstad's Grandmother)

Written by Phyllis Webstad with the help of her aunties Theresa Jack and Agness Jack, as well as her mother Rose Wilson.

Helena Mary Theresa Billy (also known as Lena) is my (Phyllis Webstad)'s grandmother. Lena was born in Dog Creek, B.C. on September 28, 1918, to Suzanne Edward Jim and biological father Moise/Moses Billy aka Billy Schwalna, who passed away when she was 9. Her step-father was George Stanislaus Jim. She was baptised on October 11, 1918.

Gran [Lena] lived at Ts'Peten, or Big Lake as we call it; the name on the map is Gustafson Lake. She lived there with her mother Suzanne and her step-dad George. George built a pit house at Ts'Peten in 1925, the same time Gran went off to school. Gran told me once that a man helped George cut the logs in half, the ends of the logs were circular, also that they made fire in the pit house and the smoke escaped through an opening in the top. It was mainly a winter home. When I asked Gran what happened to the pit house she didn't remember, nor did she remember the exact location of it at Big Lake. It wasn't until 1940 that George built a cabin above ground to replace the underground pit house.

Gran's first marriage to Moffat Jack was an arranged marriage, the last in our family. They were married on November 1, 1936 when Gran was 18 and Moffat was 32 at the St. Joseph's Mission, the same place she had previously attended Residential School for 10 years. They had five children, three who have passed on. Their surviving children are my aunt Theresa and my mother Rose.

Gran's second husband was Francis Camille. They had seven children, five of whom live today, including my aunt Agness. Gran was pregnant with my mother Rose when she and Francis united; although Francis was her step-dad, my mom always called him her dad.

Photo of Helena (Lena) Jack by Agness Jack

Gran's mother, Suzanne, was Catholic; Gran was brought up Catholic as well. They both believed strongly in the Catholic Church and said prayers daily on the Rosary. Gran attended church anytime there was a service and sang hymns. She would also smudge when offered. She would take part in the sweat lodge, which is a way of having a bath as well as a time for spiritual prayer.

Gran enjoyed working in her garden, it was something she looked forward to every Spring and it kept her strong and healthy. She grew onions, carrots, turnips, swiss chard, yellow beans, lettuce, cucumbers, tomatoes, corn, cantaloupe, and potatoes. I also remember Gran had a row of currant plants as well as rhubarb. She had many garden sites both in Dog Creek and along the Fraser River.

She also loved to be out on the land with her family travelling, camping out and berry picking. She loved to dance, I remember her dancing around the house with her arms bent toward her body, elbows in the air and she'd be dancing around. She was light on her feet as she danced, I loved watching her dance. She also enjoyed singing, like at Christmastime, a fond memory for all of us is the smell of her baking and she would be singing while she was baking.

Gran was very kind and had a gentle laugh. She had an amazing sense of humour and she loved to tell stories. When I would go visit her and she would be lying in bed, I'd lie the other way on her bed and we'd just lie there chatting away, telling stories, talking, and laughing. She was a deep thinker, she would often have her hands by her mouth, it was then that I would know she was deep in thought. I often catch myself doing the same thing at times.

Gran was brought to the Catholic run St. Joseph's Mission Residential School in 1925, she was 6-years-old, turning 7 on September 28th. There is a picture, taken during the time Gran was there, of children holding a sign that read 'Indian Mission School'. The way Gran got there was on horseback with her mother. She was the first generation in our family to attend Residential School, and the only one of her mother Suzanne's children to attend. Her mother knew that her family needed to go to school in order for her people to have a better future. Later in the year, Lena's mother would ride horseback across the countryside to visit with her for a week at Easter.

When Gran attended, half the day was learning to read, do arithmetic, and write, and the rest of the day they had to work. She learned how to make clothing and mend, how to knit, cook and bake. Gran talked about "darning the boys' socks," which meant fixing the holes in their socks. This time was also spent cleaning the convent and kitchen, baking bread, making butter and doing laundry.

She was a good seamstress. She would make dresses and make all of her kids' clothing. They were sewn by hand and the stitches would look just like a machine; you couldn't tell. Flour sacks had floral prints on them which were used to make shirts and blouses. She could take a piece of clothing, rip it apart, cut it to the appropriate size, and resew it to fit whomever it was for.

She could knit gloves with five fingers! She would also make socks. She said that knitting was like playing, it came easy to her. Later, she learned to crochet which she enjoyed. I have a blanket which she crocheted for me, I keep it tucked away for safekeeping. She tanned moose and deer hides and would then make buckskin gloves, vests, jackets, and moccasins with embroidered designs. At times, she would sell these items at the Dog Creek General Store to tourists for money.

Once, I asked Gran about any outings away from the Residential School, and she talked about going to the fall fair in Williams Lake in the back of a cattle truck. She was older when this occurred. She said that the fall fair was the only thing she went to away from the Residential School the whole time she was there, never travelled anywhere else. There were animals at the fall fair, but no carnival rides, and no special food or treats. The children each had one sweater riding in the cattle truck, some kids were so cold they could not talk.

My Mom said that Gran only talked about packing wood, making bread, knitting, and things that she did. Aunt Agness remembers that Gran was given a harmonica by one of the priests and taught how to play. Gran never talked about the bad parts or how she felt about being there. Mom said Gran had to wake up early and pack wood and throw the wood in a hole in the side of the building.

A story Gran would always tell was how her mother Suzanne sent her to school with two sweaters. When she got there, the nuns took one of her sweaters from her and gave it to another girl. That's all they had was a sweater, never a coat, so when they went on walks in the winter, they would get really cold.

Gran left Residential School in 1935 at the age of 16.

All of her ten children also attended St. Joseph's Mission, along with her two eldest grandchildren, including myself. Her great-grandson was also at the last operating Residential School in Canada that closed in

1996; my son Jeremy, his story is in this book as well.

Gran didn't have a choice, her children were taken away from her when they reached the the age of 5 or 6. When she had to let her children be taken away to Residential School, she always cried. Her children were taken away in September, some got to go home for two weeks at Christmas, and were let out for the summer in July and August. As they got older, in grade 9, they were allowed to go home at Easter for a week. The way they were transported to and from The Mission was by cattle truck, then a school bus later on. The storekeeper at Dog Creek stopped the cattle truck and insisted the children be treated better, resulting in them being transported by school bus thereafter.

Gran visited her children at The Mission during Easter, she would stay for a week. Her older children would bring her by team and wagon, traveling all night to get there. They stayed in a little log cabin near the bunkhouse where the workmen stayed, and there was a wood stove. Gran would bring her mother's dog Ringo, who would be good therapy for other kids who would play with him. Her kids ate at the dining room but spent the day at the cabin with her for the rest of the time. Gran would take part in the services, called special masses. She would bring dry fish and dry meat for her children to eat.

Gran rarely talked about feelings and emotions; it was easier to leave it alone and not talk about it. Survival was hard enough without dealing with emotions. I believe the reason she wouldn't talk about it was because she would have to relive the experiences that were very difficult. Once, when Gran was with me for the day while Mom went to town shopping she said, "If I don't want to talk about it, I won't," when I asked her more about her experience at Residential School. I knew to not ask anymore questions once she said this.

Because of her experience at Residential School, love and affection were difficult to express. The stories about this differ with my family members, some remember being hugged and told she loved them, and some do not. What I understand, and experienced, was that Gran was very loving and affectionate to babies, often carrying them on her back. A new basket was always made for the 'newcomer,' for her new grandchild or great-grandchild. She made baskets for the new babies until she was physically unable to anymore.

My aunt Agness, who I lived with when I was 9-years-old, told me that Gran was good with babies. She took good care of babies. She would hold them, feed them, rock them, sing and talk to them. But, then at about the age of 5, Gran would start to distance herself and the child. No more sitting on the lap, no more singing, no more hugging; and there were a couple of reasons for that. The first was that Gran had to prepare her heart to lose her children, child after child, year after year. The second reason for distancing that child, was to prepare that child to be in an environment where they didn't matter. When she would say "what loves it," that meant, "I love you."

My mom remembers that at Christmastime, Gran would save deer meat and put onions and spices on it to keep it until her children came home from Residential School. She could have eaten it, but she saved it for her children. She would write letters to her children but didn't share any feelings. Letters were censored before they were handed over to the children, any feelings such as 'I miss you,' were blacked out.

Her children were never whipped, she would hit the ground beside them with a willow stick but would never hit them. She would give her children a bath if they played in the ditch, she was very patient. Mom also recalls that the older kids helped the younger ones when Gran was busy or unavailable because of her work in the garden, fishing or tanning hides.

Gran made the best raisin bread pudding. We didn't get sweet stuff often, so when she would make her pudding, it was so sweet and yummy I couldn't get enough. She was also known for her homemade molasses bread and rice pudding that she would make for the Christmas bazaars. Her three youngest attended Dog Creek School, a public school, when The Mission became a 'residence' and was no longer a school. Gran always supported the Dog Creek school's fundraising efforts, doing baking, making afghans to raffle off, and buying raffle tickets.

Gran spoke English and Secwepemctsín, our Shuswap language. She was able to retain her language and this made her proud. At the Residential School, she said she spoke quietly to her friends in the language. She spoke Secwepemctsín to her children and friends who spoke fluently, but spoke English to her children and grandchildren who didn't speak the language.

The Department of Indian Affairs built Gran a house in 1965 on the Dog Creek reserve. They had to pack water from a spring above the house, or from an irrigation ditch below. I'm not sure when a well was dug and a line was put to the house for water, but I remember there was one tap with running water in the kitchen only, this was when I was 6. We did not have electricity until 1984. There was no indoor plumbing, we had to use an outhouse. My grandpa made a cellar by the house that was dug into the hillside to preserve the potatoes and canned fruits and vegetables. My Gran always kept chickens for the eggs and also had meat birds.

As a child, I only remember seeing Gran drink alcohol once. She was always there for her children and grandchildren. Like her mother, she prayed for everyone, every day; she believed strongly in the power of prayer.

In her last years, when I would visit, Gran told me many stories about her life as well as who we are related to. I'd write it down as much as I could. Sometimes, I'd have to go back to her and ask questions when I couldn't read my writing and she'd say, "I thought I told you that already," in an irritated voice. I'd tell her, "I know you did, but now I can't read my writing," and she'd laugh and answer my questions and tell me again. Another story was when she was 17. Her and her step-dad George Jim were at Big Lake, it was only the two of them there, and her step-dad got a moose. She was wanting to go home and was so mad at him, she ended up cutting it up and drying it all by herself!

In Gran's later years, she used to say that God must have forgotten about her, the same thing that her mother Suzanne used to say. She spent the last couple of years of her life at the Williams Lake Seniors Village, often only speaking in Secwepemcstín, even to the nurses who didn't understand. She could often be heard yelling, "I want lekelét!" meaning, "I want bread."

In her final hours, she quit talking, she became defensive, and she didn't want anyone close to her. Theresa says, "I'd talk in Shuswap and she would finally hold my hand. I knew she was crying; she was sad because she knew she was leaving."

Gran passed away surrounded by family on the morning of January 19, 2019. She is buried in the Dog Creek cemetery. Her funeral service was conducted by a Secwépemc Elder and was a combination of Catholic and Secwépemc prayers. People that attended the funeral were many of Gran's immediate family, her relatives and friends, as well as band members who respected her throughout her long life.

Now I know what is meant when people say, "always in my heart." Gran, you will always be in my heart, you are greatly missed. We love you and will always remember you. I will make sure that the future generations know about you and your life story.

Gran was good with babies…but then at about the age of 5, Gran would start to distance herself and the child…there were a couple of reasons for that. The first was that Gran had to prepare her heart to lose her children, child after child, year after year. The second reason for distancing that child, was to prepare that child to be in an environment where they didn't matter.

A hand beaded flower earring; this was the last beadwork Gran made before her passing, she was never able to complete the other earring.

A cardinal pin that was a favourite of Gran's; she loved cardinals.

Rose Wilson nee Jack
(Phyllis Webstad's Mother)

I am Rose Wilson (nee Jack) from the Stswecem'c/Xgat'tem First Nation (Canoe Creek/Dog Creek). My parents are Lena Billy and Moffat Jack. My step-father, whom I called Dad, was Francis Camille. My maternal grandparents were Suzanne Jim and Moise Billy from Canoe Creek, B.C. My step-grandfather, my Granny's second husband, was George Jim. My paternal grandparents were Lucie William from Esket, B.C., and Jean Baptiste William from Sugar Cane, B.C.

Life Before Residential School

My mother and father's marriage was an arranged marriage, the last one in the history of my family. Together they had 5 children, I am the youngest. Mom was pregnant with me when she separated from my father and got with my step-dad.

We didn't live on reserve, my mom and dad didn't have their own house. We lived at Francis Meadow in a log cabin that my dad built. Someone burned it down, so he then built another cabin made of lumber. That's where we lived until Mom got a house in Dog Creek in 1965. Before, when we visited the reserve in Dog Creek, we went to our grandma Suzanne's place because she had a home there. We travelled with the seasons. In the summer, we would be up at my dad's meadow, or down at the river picking berries or fishing for salmon. And in the fall, we would be out hunting and up on Dog Creek Mountain, and out on the territory hunting wild meat. That's what I miss today, the wild meat. We had porcupine, and moose, deer, grouse — a lot of that, and trout from the creek at Gustafson Lake. That lake was made by my people, it's their own lake that they made. What I remember about porcupine is it had a lot of fat, my mom just loved it. She always wanted a porcupine. Now you hardly see that kind of meat around.

I spoke English, my mom taught me, she spoke both English and our language growing up. I was always around our Elders who spoke our language. We would visit my aunts and uncles on the reserve and they were speaking our language. Young people now have to go to a classroom to learn our language, it was all around me when I was growing up.

Day Taken

I had six-years-nine-months of loving, carefree years being at home around Dog Creek and Canoe Creek area. Then, sometime in early September 1954, I was sent to St. Joseph's Mission, south of Williams Lake, B.C. The Mission was also known as Caribou Indian Residential School. My dad Francis didn't want to let us go. He's my step-dad, but I call him my dad because he was there from the day I was born. He never did tell me I am not your father; he was always there.

I remember getting there [to Residential School], getting out of the vehicle, and looking for something or someone familiar. I saw my older sister Theresa and I ran over to her, and she chased me away. She didn't want to play with me and I felt bad. I met my friend, you have to have a buddy when you're there, you have to have someone you can talk to.

Bed and Food

For sleeping, we had dormitories. It was a big area, like a gym, juniors, and intermediates, and seniors each had a dormitory. Boys were on one side and girls on another, we weren't allowed to talk to our brothers and sisters. I remember some of the boys used to come into our dorm and see their girlfriends, they would sneak in and see them. We weren't allowed to curl our hair so we had to learn to do our hair in the dark when the lights went out at 9:00.

The food, oh my, until about grade 6 it was yucky. It was what we called slop and they would mix spoiled milk with our porridge and expect us to eat that, it wasn't appetizing. There was a cook who came in and he gave us better food. He taught me how to bake cookies and cake, that's grade 7 when we got better meals. I remember watching the food go by and the staff would be getting bacon and eggs and toast and we would have porridge and bread. Our bread wasn't toasted, just bread with a bit of butter. Once in a while, we got peanut butter or jam. When we would be playing and skipping, we'd be singing about 'mush potato slop'.

Day to Day Life at Residential School

We learned to do some activities that took up the time spent at the Residential School. The good times were spent playing with my buddies...

[one of which] was my best friend. On Saturday nights, we all, all the boys and girls, plus the staff, watched movies on a big screen. Sometimes we had skating parties and after the skating party, we had hot chocolate. We also had picnics at Rocky Point or Yellow Lake, or across the Highway 97 backwoods. I liked swimming in the huge pool. We also played softball.

Girls had to learn how to do clothes mending and also mending socks. I learned how to use a sewing machine. When I was in grade 9, I made myself a beautiful pink dress. The dress was pink with colourful flowers on the fabric, I wore that dress for Easter mass in 1962. I didn't like getting up early to go to mass. Around Easter it was hard getting up early before breakfast at about 6:00, then chapel at about 7:00.

People working at the school, some were funny, some were mean. My two friends were daredevils and they would be getting me to go along with them, to follow them. The Mission had boundaries, we had to stay in the playground. My friends were like, "Come on let's go!", and we would be walking arm in arm up to the road where we were not supposed to go, and my two friends would be giggling. A nun would be running up behind us, "You girls come back here!", it was funny. I remember there was a long bench and we would all be standing on it in front of the nun. I remember that it broke in half and it looked so funny, her face went so red. Things like that, there were good and bad times.

From the time I came to the Residential School, we learned how to thoroughly do housework — washing dishes, cleaning the shower areas, a row of face washing sinks, and the bathroom floors. One good thing that happened to me when I was 13-years-old, the chef noticed how clean and shiny I kept the dishwashing room and big counters, so he invited me into the bakery. He showed one of my friends and I how to bake and we baked cakes and cookies for all the staff and children.

Punishment

I behaved myself the best way I knew how. I hardly got into trouble. My buddies were the instigators, I was the follower. We weren't allowed to visit anyone after the lights went out. I was 12-years-old, an intermediate, when I was whispering away with my chum when the light came on and the nun said, "Who's that whispering?" We must have been whispering loud. I admitted that it was me. The nun made me kneel in the large aisle. She forgot about me. In the wee hours of the morning, I finally got into my bed.

There were rules, and when you broke them, you had to stand in the corner or kneel in the aisle. I remember being strapped but I don't remember what it was for, but it hurt because they used a ruler or a leather strap. I knew right from wrong and I tried my best to behave. I didn't like being strapped so I tried my best to obey the rules.

When I first started school, I used to wet my bed. It was humiliating. The supervisor would put my stinky, wet bed sheet on my head in front of the other children to see and taunt.

I am not a fighter. I had encountered bullies. I felt ashamed to tell the bully that I don't want to fight. I got out of the situation.

I never did try to leave because I saw what happened to others who tried. The boys who they brought back had to wear dresses, or else they shaved their heads. I can't remember what they did to the girls. I never tried to run away because they just brought you back anyway, you can't get away, and I didn't want to be punished for it.

Visits With Family

I missed my family terribly. My mom would write and she would tell us about our new member of the family when a new brother or sister would be born. I would wish I could be there with them, my younger siblings, when they would do little things, when they would walk and things like that. I missed out on so much. When I went home we would clean their faces and be glad to be with them.

I got to go home at Christmas, and in grade 8 they let us go home at Easter. At the end of June, they would let us go for the summer. When we got to go home, we had horses. [We were] out on the land, up at the meadow, or visiting our relatives, a few days at each place. My aunt and uncle had a big garden in Canoe Creek, sometimes we would get a moose or a deer from them.

When I got older, about 14 or 15, me and my younger siblings went to work picking fruit in Sumas, USA. After the Williams Lake Stampede, which is always at the end of June and early July, the owner of the fruit farm in Sumas would pick up workers. He had a bus and would bring us there to work; a couple of times he even would bring us back to Williams Lake when we were done working for him. The welfare worker on the reserve didn't want to give Mom money for us to buy food and clothing. So before we went back to school we had to go to work and pick fruit.

The bus from The Mission would pick up and drop us off at the top of the hill before going down into the Dog Creek Reserve. Dog

Creek's Shuswap name is Xgat'tem, which means Deep Valley. Mom and Dad would have to meet the bus with their sleigh or wagon because the bus had a hard time with mountainous roads. The road into the reserve is a dirt road, steep, and would be either icy, muddy, or filled with snow.

When we would see our parents in the summer, Christmas, or Easter, it was hard to leave and hard to think of when we would see them again. The first few days after we got back to The Mission after being at home, we'd quietly sit around. We didn't want to run around and play, we'd just sit there. We missed home and our parents, little siblings left behind at home, grandmother, and the rest of our loved ones on the reserve.

Life After Residential School

I was there [at Residential School] for 10 years, I left in June 1964. When I left that year, I remember waiting and waiting for my mom and dad to come and get me by taxi from Williams Lake. Everyone was leaving and I was crying. There was a bus that was picking up everyone else to bring them back to the reserve. My uncle and grandma got me to get on the bus with them and my sister because I was scared to be left alone. I guess when my mom and dad did finally come to get me, I wasn't there. I didn't get to go home with mom and dad until we met up with them while picking berries down at the river.

I am glad that I survived those 10 years at The Mission. I am happy that all my siblings survived as well. All of us are accounted for, there is no one missing.

Shortly after leaving The Mission, I had my baby at age 20. Her name is Phyllis. I wanted so much to stay home and look after her. I received a letter from the Indian Agent office telling me that I didn't have any responsibilities and that I should go out and work. We had to listen to the Indian Agent or go to jail. How could I get a job when I barely had grade 10? I was too shy to be a waitress. I ended up leaving Phyllis with Mom and I went to the USA to work in the cannery or picking fruit. The Band welfare couldn't even give me $80.00/month for my daughter and I. Nowadays, welfare helps single mothers.

Effects

The Residential School seemed like a prison sentence, it felt like I was never going to get out of there. I was there for 10 years. I didn't understand why I was sent to Residential School at first, but then I learned they [my parents] would be sent to jail for not sending us there. They would take my mom or dad away because they wouldn't let them take us away to school. I've never fully understood why some had to go to Residential School and some didn't from our reserve. My one uncle gave up his Indian Status so his children wouldn't have to go to the Residential School. He and his family lived on the border of the reserve in a log cabin. He couldn't live on the reserve because he and his children was considered to be no longer an Indian.

Mom went to Residential School. She never talked about the bad parts, just the good things like what she learned. She learned how to play harmonica over there, she learned from a Brother how to play. One good thing was that we learned how to do things like baking and sewing, we would mend clothing, like children's clothing. In my mom's day, they learned to make things like gloves and shirts, we didn't learn that. The only thing we didn't learn, well, was about life skills. When you come out into the real world, when you come out, it's different. I felt so free, and I felt sorry for myself, and I didn't know how to conduct myself. I just started drinking and drinking. I tried marijuana, but it wasn't for me. I was lucky, they have different kinds of drugs nowadays, like fentanyl, we didn't have that.

So I had an angel or two on my side. I wasn't sexually abused, but it's just as bad to be psychologically abused, they put the fear in you so bad, not to step out of line. Residential School affected me in that I felt like I had no voice, and I was afraid to express my opinions, and what I thought wasn't important. They didn't want us to express ourselves, we just had to listen and do what they wanted you to do. You had to listen or else, the strap, or I heard that some people were put in a dungeon and made them stay there for days. I was pretty lucky nothing really drastic happened to me, I learned about it later, the abuse and that.

I turned into a practicing alcoholic addict. During my sober moments, circumstances happened. When I turned 30, I got married to a non-Indian. As a result, I lost my status. In later years when women could be reinstated Natives, my letter came back stating that I am an Indian of Canada. I wrote back and asked to be reinstated back to Canoe Creek Band.

I didn't make good choices when I was in my alcoholic addict years. But once I turned my life around, I promised myself that for the second half of my life I would look for the good in things. I had to reprogram my mind.

Healing and Recovery

In 1991 I went to cooking school. I was 40 by then and realizing I needed to sober up if I was going to make it through cooking school.

When I first decided to quit drinking, I was reaching out for help. I couldn't get drunk anymore and I didn't want to get involved in hard stuff. I went to the North Shore Friendship Centre in Kamloops, the counsellor wasn't in and I went home and I cried and cried because no one was there to help me. I didn't want to go back to drinking. I knelt down at my bed, and I prayed, and I talked to myself. The only one that can help me is me, it was really hard to do.

I went to alcohol program meetings, it was hard. I knew I had to sober up to make it through cooking school. It took me a long time to get where I wanted to be. I made it through, I promised myself I would stay sober enough to get through the course. By the time I graduated it had given me enough time to think and to realize that I needed to stay sober if I wanted to get and keep a job. Shortly after, I checked myself into the Maple Ridge drug and alcohol treatment centre.

I was sober 8 years before I went to a healing program for Residential School Survivors on Vancouver Island called Tsow-Tun-Le Lum. It was a big step for me. I cried and cried when I knew what I had to do next. I didn't think that Residential School had really affected me and I wasn't treated as bad as some other people. But when you hear what happened to other people, it hurt you just as much, to listen to other people's pain, it was really hard. I was crying and I was happy and sad at the same time. I had to go through it, the pain, to be happy, too. I was there for 28 days, which was supposed to be 6 weeks but the government cut it back.

As I rethink my Residential School years, I didn't know how much it had impacted me until I went to Tsow-Tun-Le Lum. With my Tsow-Tun-Le Lum peers, we shared with one another our experiences, cried together, and our counsellors were there for us. I liked the medicine woman and her helpers the best. She is the strongest spiritual person that I ever ran across. She took a lot of bad stuff off of me.

I'd always wanted to get my grade 12. At Residential School, Father, who was also the principal, used to tell me that I would never go beyond grade 9. I needed to prove him wrong. One of the course requirements was a grade 11 First Nation studies course. Even after all of my healing work, it still hurt to face the Residential School thing again in that course. I just cried when I looked at the questions I had to answer. I was finally able to get my Adult Dogwood Grade 12 equivalency. I've also taken other training such as Life Skills and Home Support Resident Care Aide. I am also a member of an alcoholics fellowship program.

Today, I am more aware of why I do the things I do. I read self-help books on why the brain works the way that it does, and I took other training, learning about how to interact with people and how to understand myself and others. I learned why I was drinking and how to cope. I live in Kamloops, B.C. now. I miss gardening, I don't have a garden here. Gardening is why my mom lived so long, gardening and tanning hides. Mom lived to be 100. She made buckskin coats, she was really good at everything including beading, and she used to make sweaters too.

What I would like people to know about Residential School or First Nations people in Canada. No matter how bleak things seem to be, like for me it took me a long time to see that there's good in the world. When I sobered up I told myself I would look for the good in the world for the rest of my life, because the other way doesn't work. When I was drinking I didn't see any other way until I sobered up. I was 40 and I promised myself that for the second half of my life I would look for the good in things and not dwell on the past but keep going ahead. That's what I learned anyway. I pray for my grandchildren, that they will have a good sober journey.

> *"Shortly after leaving The Mission, I had my baby at age 20. Her name is Phyllis. I wanted so much to stay home and look after her. I received a letter from the Indian Agent office telling me that I didn't have any responsibilities and that I should go out and work. We had to listen to the Indian Agent or go to jail."*

Tsow-Tun-Le Lum is a fully accredited, registered, non-profit treatment society in Lantzville, on Vancouver Island.

Theresa Jack
(Phyllis Webstad's Auntie)

I am Theresa Jack, my mother was Lena Jack, my father was Moffat Jack, and my grandmother was Suzanne Edward Jim. I was born on July 11 1945. I went to St. Joseph's Mission Indian Residential School from age 7 in 1952, to age 16 in 1961.

Life Before Residential School

My brother Morris, my sister Victorine aka Vicky, and I were sent to live with my grandmother Suzanne, after my parents separated when I was one year old. Morris and I were never allowed to go visit our Mom, but Vicky was allowed to go where she wanted.

Granny Suzanne looked after us. She was old when she got us, but she did everything for us. She bathed us, washed and combed our hair, and washed our clothes, all by hand. There was no running water or electricity and we had an outhouse. She made sure we had a quarter when we went to Canoe Creek for church because they had a collection, and she made sure we were dressed when we travelled by horse. I was the smallest and she made me ride behind her, which I didn't like. I was strapped right behind her and my head was covered with her blanket.

There was lots of drinking and violence on the reserve. Many times at Granny Suzanne's, we had to hide outside for our safety, usually in the sweat house or the haystack by the creek. My two uncles lived with us. One of them abused me sexually, and the other abused me mentally and physically. He would beat me and my brother with sticks and anything he could get his hands on. He even bullwhipped us once. I'd be so scared I'd pee myself and he would whip me more. I know we needed discipline, but not that harsh. By the time I went to Residential School, I was really tough and couldn't cry.

When I was 7, Granny Suzanne brought me to watch my brother and sister get picked up to go to Residential School. Morris was 8 and Vicky was 11. They took me as well. The trip to the Residential

School was two hours long. We made that trip in a cattle truck. I remember a nun riding with us and making us say Catholic prayers all the way to the Residential School. They said Granny cried all the way home because they picked me up; she wasn't expecting me to get taken.

Day Taken

I was crying when I got off the cattle truck at The Mission because I didn't know where I was, and I didn't know anyone. Then, I saw my cousin and another girl I knew. My cousin is the same age as me so we hugged each other and felt better. We were support for each other. We talked Secwepemctsín; it was all we knew.

I heard that in the past, some were beaten for speaking their language but that didn't happen to us while I was there. We were each given a relative to teach us English as none of the young ones spoke English. An older cousin was assigned to look after me and help me to learn English. They would ask me my name and she'd tell me to say, "Number 65." That was my number. Our number was just like our own name. I had number 65 until I left The Mission. Once, they tried to give my number away to someone else but I fought for it and I kept it. I threw out the girl's stuff from my locker 65, I hollered to them, "I own that number, no one is going to take it from me!"

Day to Day Life

Our hair was cut short, up to the ears, and with short bangs. I think they cut our hair like that so that it would be easier to get rid of head lice, and easier to clean. On weekends, we had to sit around with that DDT in our hair and clean each others' hair of lice.

We only were allowed to take showers, never a bath. There was only one tub, and the only one allowed to have a bath had a head injury and used to faint. Even now, I don't like to have a shower because it reminds me of The Mission.

We had to wear a tam and a dress all the time. We had uniforms and weren't allowed to wear pants. We took off the uniform after school and wore regular clothes with an apron over it. We had to wear an apron all the time. At home, Granny always made sure we wore our tam.

In grade 4, after school, we had to mend the boys' clothes on the sewing machine and darn socks. I remember one girl tried to take short-cuts and they just ripped it up and she had to do it over. If it wasn't done properly, the Sister would make us take it apart and do it again. So we had to do it right and we learned to mend. When we finished sewing we got to do embroidery, which I loved. We had hobby nights, craft nights, for an hour. I learned to do beading, which I also like.

If we got sick or hurt, the Sisters nursed us. If there was some-thing wrong, they would fix it. Sister Delores and Sister Albina were nurses. I used to talk to Sister Albina about my parents' divorce, why I didn't live with them, and how I didn't like it when they would ask about my parents. I would cry and tell Sister about how I just had my granny.

At Residential School we would do stuff. We went on picnics, we played baseball and other sports, we watched hockey on weekends, and we had skating parties in the winter. We went tobogganing and we all helped each other carry the boards back up the hill, so that was fun. I froze my feet once and they gave me an extra chocolate. My feet were really frozen and I was crying; I guess they wanted to make me feel better.

We had a 12-inch black and white TV mounted up on the wall. We would sit on the cement floor and watch Ed Sullivan, Hootenanny, and all those old shows. We liked that, and sometimes one of the priests would play Elvis and rock and roll on his guitar. He'd play and we'd dance. We loved dancing. We had sock hops on Friday and we'd really dance.

We had chores at The Mission. We had to clean the priests' rooms and pack long pieces of wood for the furnace downstairs where we slept. That was where we went to school, too. I was really smart in school. I used to come first, second, or third in spelling, reading, and writing until I left.

I liked being at The Mission because I felt safe, with all the drink-ing, violence, and abuse at home. Residential School was good for me because it taught me everything. It taught me how to care for people, I have been a caretaker since I was 7, I grew up fast. I looked after my family. We were taught to care for people. We had a lot of resilience and I still have it yet.

Living Arrangements

There was a long outhouse that fit about six kids in 1953, when I first started. Then they got flushing toilets when we moved to the new building. We had to move our beds to the new building, and we were happy. The boys' building burned, and the Father's little house did as well. At the new building, there was a fence separating the boys and the girls.

We were allowed to visit, at the fence. My younger cousin was always at the fence because he was lonely. I used to get tired of going to visit him but I did because I knew he was lonely.

Punishment

I got into trouble at The Mission. My friend, she became a cop later, and I had to go to her for counselling. She would ask me, "What trouble have you got yourself into now?" And we just laughed because she and I got into so much trouble at The Mission. We always misbehaved or talked when we weren't supposed to talk, and we would get a spanking. I couldn't feel it so I had to fake it and cry because I was so tough from being beat-up and bullwhipped at home.

I ran away once with my two friends. We were trying to get to 150 Mile [House] to get some snuff. We went through the bush, but we didn't know where we were going. It was noon so we went back because we were hungry. If you ran away, they would cut your hair short and make you wear a gunny sack dress, and boys got their hair shaved off. My brother was one year older than I was. He stole some carrots from the garden, and they shaved all of his hair off for that.

My best friend died there in grade 8. He was a nice student, really friendly. He sat in front of me and we always talked together. One day he didn't come back. They said he died. He had kidney problems and he died. So after that, they told us to report it if we were sick. I always think of my friend. A lot of kids went missing in those days. In the older days, they didn't do anything about it, but now they might. Some kids ran away when it was really cold and they froze to death.

Food

I didn't like the [Government of Canada's] apology in 2008 because they never gave us enough money for the hell we went through. We were fed bad food. When I was in grade 9, they made us eat spoiled milk and mush slop we threw away. The cook, a white guy, told us we had to eat it before we could go. An older girl told us in Shuswap not to listen, to just stand there and don't eat it. Some got sick, throwing up just looking at that garbage, and we stood there for a long time before they let us go. One of the cooks used to cook with a smoke in his mouth and I'm sure the ashes fell into our food. While I was there, I never heard of food allergies.

We didn't have much food and if we didn't like it, that's all we had. We would steal food like bread and give it to the little kids and to my younger siblings.

Staff got bacon and eggs, but we got mush, and hamburger sometimes, with lots of gravy. When I was in grade 9 they started bringing out better food, like meatballs, fruit, and apples for our snack. We would sometimes get an orange on weekends. Some would play catch with it for days. They didn't want to eat it, they wanted to save it. I remember coffee during a picnic, a huge pot. We would stand around the fire and dip in until it was gone. The first time I remember having rice was when I went to Prince George for Grade 10. In Grade 9, Granny sent a big box of bread and stuff on The Stage for us.

There was a canteen open on weekends, for those whose parents sent them money. We had to get in line just for a handful of candy. Mom would send me money and I'd share with my siblings when I got candy. A chocolate would have been 5 or 10 cents.

The workers at The Mission had dogs. They didn't come around to where we were so we were never able to pet them. The Mission had cattle that were looked after away from the main buildings, but we never got steak, just hamburger.

Visits With Family

We went home at Christmas and in summertime. It was good to be home with my grandmother. She never went to school, and she made the best bread. I don't know how she learned because she couldn't read or write, but she could make the best bread. The older people were really good at baking and doing things for survival. And when I got old enough, I told my uncle that bullwhipped me that I wasn't a little kid anymore when he tried to beat me up, and I really beat him up!

Once we were in grade 9, we were also allowed to go home for Easter. While I was at home for Easter, Granny got me to make lots of cake to bring back to my younger siblings. I put thick chocolate icing on the cakes because I knew they would like that.

Birthdays weren't celebrated at The Mission, but they weren't celebrated at home either. We didn't have presents at Christmas. We had chicken at Christmas, and I don't remember wanting anything else. We didn't know about presents. As long as we had a home and something to eat we were happy. We didn't have anything for Halloween when I was younger at The Mission. Later on, though, I remember they put apples in a big tub and we had to put our head in there and bite the apple. It was called apple bobbing. We also had candied apples, we liked that.

Life After Residential School

When I went to high school at Williams Lake in grade 9, my grades went downhill but they passed me anyway. I went to [school in] Prince George in grade 10 when I was 16. I was never given any money for school, I had to work and buy my own clothes and stuff. I quit after Christmas holidays because I found out my mother was having a bad time. She was nearly barefoot, dragging wood for the winter fire from the creek. My siblings were all little so I quit school and went to work to help buy groceries and clothing for them. That's when stuff was so cheap we could buy anything. At Stampede, I got my younger siblings each a hat and boots. I worked at Circle S Ranch, gardening and everything to buy clothes and food for the kids. One hundred fifty dollars would get a wagon load of stuff from the general store in Dog Creek.

I can still speak Shuswap, I had to talk to my mother in Shuswap when she was dying. She was pushing people away. She didn't want people to get too close, so I talked to her in Shuswap and she felt better. She held my hands with two hands and she was happy. Her eyes were far away, probably because of the morphine she had to take for her pain. She was under the drug, even at the end, I just held her hand and I prayed and sang for her. I didn't know she was gone. I felt the electric from her hand so I thought she was still there; my niece Phyllis told me she was gone. I went up to her bedside and I really cried. It's the last time I cried so much because I knew she was gone.

I didn't hear about the bad stuff happening in Residential School until I finished school. I didn't know it was happening, even to my closest friends; they didn't talk about it. I guess we were not allowed to talk about anything in those days, we had to keep everything inside.

But I think mostly the Residential School taught us a lot of stuff, right and wrong. They taught us a lot of good things so I liked it, but there was also a lot of bad stuff. They taught us the Bible and stuff, but they were doing all those bad things.

I know I don't want to be treated like I was at The Mission, but I guess we needed discipline. I disciplined my kids with an iron hand but I never spanked them. They are older, but if they step out of line, I still tell them. If I didn't care I wouldn't, but I do care. I have a lot of resilience and patience. I can wait and wait. There's another tomorrow unless I am in a hurry. We learned survival skills along with reading, writing, and math. We had to learn it 100%. But, some of our people suffered from abuse in there. And that wasn't good, they are still dying from drugs and alcohol on the street. They're lost.

It must have been worse when they [The Mission] first started, really bad, like a concentration camp. My mother went for 8 years and they kept her for 2 extra years to do baking and wash by hand. Mostly she told us the good things. They didn't have shoes; they went everywhere barefoot. They must have been tough. I don't know what they wore in the winter. We had everything when we went to school, but those in Mom's age didn't have anything. She liked some stuff, too. She talked about baseball, she loved it. I think we got our strength from our mother. She learned everything, and she was a go-getter.

I can make clothes because I learned to sew, mend, and do beading at The Mission. I make regalia for my family and I am a pretty good artist if I have to draw. I think that's what kept me alive, being positive all these years. There were times when I didn't want to go on, but I remembered to think positive. I think that's what kept my mother going as well. She was 100, she would start to feel down and we would pray and then she would feel better, she would be all smiles. Get her to think positive and she would feel better. With all this stuff happening these days we have to think positive and be Survivors.

Some people left our church, and I was going to leave because of the priests and what they did to the other kids. But then I thought, it wasn't the Creator that did that, it was his workers, so I kept going to church. But I didn't like what was going on. I learned about it on the news on TV. The priests were denying everything, some of the victims couldn't step forward because they were ashamed. I watched a show about the abuse. It was so hard to watch, my stomach turned. After, I was so weak I couldn't walk. It was so scary, even though it didn't happen to me, that so many kids, including those in my own family, got abused.

I don't miss the priests. I pray in my own dwelling, my own home. My mother told us we have to pray, people are trying to kill us, but prayers are powerful. I've been praying all the time, every day. I think that's what saved me, when my mother went I almost went ahead of her. When I had pneumonia, I nearly quit breathing twice, but I got my breath back. They took me to emergency and put me under oxygen but I survived. The Residential School made us Survivors. I didn't like their discipline but we needed the discipline. That's what I tell my son, everywhere you go you get disciplined so you have to listen.

As First Nations, we are the keepers of this land, but now we don't have our land. We have a little place and it's nothing but rocks. They took all our land and gave us rocks. Now we are trying to get it back, but they sold the best land for ranches and stuff. To be a Native, you have to be resilient and strong, you have to stand up for your rights and everything.

"Birthdays weren't celebrated at The Mission, but they weren't celebrated at home either. We didn't have presents at Christmas. We had chicken at Christmas, and I don't remember wanting anything else. We didn't know about presents. As long as we had a home and something to eat, we were happy."

Hazel Agness Jack
(Phyllis Webstad's Auntie)

My name is Hazel Agness Jack, I am from Canoe Creek/Dog Creek Band (Stswe-cem'c/ Xgat'tem). I choose to go by my middle name, Agness.

My mother is Lena Jack and my father is Francis Camille. My maternal grandparents are Suzanne Edward Jim and George Jim. My paternal grandparents are Old Camille and Agnes Kalelest.

Life Before Residential School

I remember a lot of times with my mom and dad, travelling by horse and wagon or on horseback. When we rode, my Dad would tie us on the saddle to keep us on. I loved horseback riding. I remember my mother berry picking, she carried me on her back wrapped in a blanket when I was a year old. I remember sitting on the floor in my granny's house, watching her dance around as she hummed to herself, or she would grab our hands and dance around with us. I remember her baking yeast bread and eating a bun with homemade jam. I remember my granny leading the prayers in the church, even when the priest wasn't there.

Being with my parents, I always felt safe and felt good being out on the land. I remember Dad's meadow, called Francis Meadow. Mom and dad fishing, hunting, drying meat and fish, trapping and tanning hides, doing traditional activities. At Spring Gulch, Tsewew'xe, there was a communal garden where the Band members planted potatoes. Whoever happened by would spend a day or two to cultivate and irrigate the garden.

My older sister went to Residential School. She came home from school with new games and singing skipping songs. My three older siblings, I didn't know too well as they lived with our grandmother, Suzanne Edwards Jim, my mom's mother.

[I remember when] welfare, it was called 'relief', was intro-

Photo of Agness Jack by Darrin Andrews.

duced, it was a devastating time for our people. Up until then, my parents took care of our needs, in terms of food gathered, they worked as a team to support the family. 'Relief' changed all that for everyone. It was given to the women, so the men as providers 'had the rug pulled out from under them' as I saw it.

I remember good things about my mom and my dad, aunts, uncles, and cousins. Mom taught us to look out for each other, help each other out. Older children looked after the younger ones. We fished for trout in the spring at Big Lake as we called it, on the map, it is known as Gustafsen lake. We would go camping up there. I remember my dad trapping muskrat, my mom setting her squirrel snares. The fish spawn in the creeks in the springtime. My brother held one net in the creek and I held another net, while my mother chased fish into my net. The fish wouldn't try to swim out of the net, they would just keep filling the net. I was worried that as the net got heavy, I would drop it and I would lose all the fish. And all of the sudden my mom would come out of nowhere and grab the net and dump the fish on the shore, away from the creek. Then she would reset the net and off she would go. Our dog Buster, a black lab, would grab a fish and drop the fish off at my pile or my brother's. That dog was our protector.

Day Taken

I didn't know it, but when I went to the Residential School the police had taken my dad to Oakalla prison in Vancouver, I think. That's another part of our history that needs to be told. Oakalla is where people ended up when they were arrested for being drunk on the street or broke the Indian Act policies.

I went to school when I was 6-years-old. I know that because that's when I got my first shots, 1956, at Residential School. I arrived in October. It was 2 hours from Dog Creek to Residential School outside of 150 Mile House. I was at my granny's with my mother when Terry Thompson who ran the store drove up to my granny's house, which was unusual because he usually parked on the road and we walked up to the Dog Creek Stage, a panel truck that took us to town. My mom brought my brother and I out after getting us washed up and dressed in clean clothes. Terry Thompson drove a panel truck, my brother and I sat in the seat behind him, I wondered why my mother wasn't coming. My mother and granny watched us leave. He brought us right to The Mission. The truck had no windows in the back so we didn't really get to see anything.

My brother and I were both wondering what was going on. I remember coming around the corner and seeing the big white building. I knew about prison and I remember thinking we're going to prison, we're going to jail. Somebody must have described what prison looked like to me at one time.

My older sisters came out to meet us. My brother was taken to the boys' side. My sisters probably explained to me that I was there to go to school, but all I really remember was feeling so alone and afraid. I wanted to cry but couldn't. My sister Theresa gave me hard candies, but with the lump in my throat, I didn't feel like putting the candies in my mouth so I just held them in my right hand. We were marched into the dining room and I remember thinking how am I going to eat with these candies in my hand. My sister took them out of my hand which was dyed red from the candies. I remember just sitting in the dining hall with all the spoons and forks hitting the plates and all the chatter. It was different for me to hear all the people-noise. I looked to see where my brother Clarence was but I didn't see him. I remember being so lonely and just wanting to be back with my mom and dad. I realized I was stuck there. I didn't like the way the nuns looked in their black habits, and the priests in their long black robes.

I got really sick before Christmas that year. It turned out I had tuberculosis (TB) so I couldn't go home for Christmas. I remember being sick in the infirmary and feeling very alone. I was so weak and sick that I couldn't climb up on my bed. The following spring, I was taken to a TB hospital where I spent the next four years. I missed my family, but we were treated a lot better in Coqualeetza Indian Hospital than we were at The Mission.

Bed and Food

It always seemed cold climbing into bed. It took a long time to warm up and go to sleep. You would hear other girls crying, I probably cried too but I don't remember. I remember little girls getting into trouble because they peed their beds. I could understand why they peed their beds because the bed was so cold when you got into bed. That wasn't our experience at home. I remember hearing the crying in the dorm at night and that was hard. As a little girl, I could understand why they cried, missing home and not liking being there.

Milk tasted gross, I think it was actually powdered milk. They gave us cod liver oil after school. We would line up by age groups and were given a squirt of cod liver oil on our tongues. Later, it was a black cod liver pill which we would hold under our tongue and spit it out when we went outside to play. Fish was a big part of our diet at home. We definitely lived healthier at home than at The Mission. They grew potatoes at The Mission but they sold the best potatoes. The potatoes we were given were grey-looking and there were big chunks of cooked turnips. I hate cooked turnips to this day. We called the food 'slop'. I remember skipping games, older girls chanting skipping songs, mashed potatoes and slop were a part of the song.

Relationships

I found the nuns very uncaring, very cold. Mean. Things I had never experienced of adults before Residential School, because they say a community raises a child, that is how I felt as a child. There were always adults around keeping an eye on us, making sure that we didn't do anything harmful, anything where we could get hurt. My aunts, and uncles, and grandmother, they were all a part of my life and they would let us know if we were doing something that we shouldn't, but they never did it in a mean way, they never spanked us or treated us roughly. Not like at The Mission where a nun would grab your arm and spin you around if they wanted to talk to you, they were pretty mean. And I was never called by my name Hazel, I was called by a number. Most times at home, I was called Helly. My brother couldn't say my name and would pronounce it as Helly, everyone called me Helly because of that. We never did see the boys, only in the classroom, or the chapel, or outside, but there was an invisible boundary line which we could not cross. I wanted so bad to be away from that place.

There were cliques. After being in the TB sanatorium, going back to Residential School was a shock to me, going back to that social situation. I wasn't supposed to be friends with my sister's enemies, or because they were Chilcotin or Carrier, but I was one of the few to have friends in all the three tribal groups. There were also individuals from the Lillooet or St'at'imc Nation at The Mission. I chose to ignore the unspoken rules and I was ostracized because I was indifferent to those unspoken rules.

Language

We were fluent in Secwépemc (Shuswap Language). Our mother taught us numbers, colours, and prayers in English before we went to school. We would use our language when the nuns weren't around.

Punishment

When I went back to The Mission from Coqualeetza Indian Hospital I was in grade five. Mother Superior, who was the head of the nuns, would come down to the play-hall on Saturday evening and the nuns would give her a list of names and call the girls up to the front of the line. We would already be in line to see a movie that was played on Saturday nights. Mother Superior would call us up, and I remember that she called my name once. She had this strap that had a wire on the end that was a hook they would hang it up with. You would hold out your hands and you would get the strap.

One of my friends had told me that just before the strap hits, you tighten your palm, and when the strap hits it won't hurt as much, so that's what I did. And then the strap hits you between your palm and where your elbow bends. I found out later, that was one place that you didn't bruise when you got hit and that's why they strapped us there. They didn't tell you what you were getting the strap for and if you asked, you were given more. To this day I don't know what I got the strap for. My oldest sister Theresa asked me what I was getting the strap for, and what hurt the most was Theresa reprimanding me for not knowing what I was getting the strap for.

We learned that a group punishment was better than an individual's punishment. So when something happened, we wouldn't tell the nuns, who wanted us to point out the person or persons who were fighting or breaking whatever rules. The group punishment was done in the play-hall where we had to kneel on the cement floor, always by age group. And after about an hour or half an hour, the little girls would go to bed and Mother Superior would walk in and give us a lecture. I don't remember her lectures. I would zone out and my mind would be elsewhere. I would be in my memories of home, I wouldn't listen to Mother Superior who would pace back and forth, once in a while I would bring my mind back to the play-hall. The group punishment was better in our eyes than watching the girls get punished individually.

I remember when a couple of my friends ran away, we were in grade six. When they brought them back to The Mission, they would have their hair shaved off with some left for bangs along the front. The girls would wear a kerchief around their heads in the dining hall, the chapel, and in the classroom, but when they were in the company of just us girls they weren't allowed to wear it. They were probably very humiliated but we never teased them or anything. My half-brother George Sargent was sent to Residential School by his mom because she wanted him to learn how to read. He ran away three times, and by the third time, they didn't bother bringing him back. I had asked him if he went to school because I would see him reading sometimes when I visited him.

Visits With Family

My mother always came at Eastertime and spent about a week. My dad never came there. We were home for a couple of weeks at Christmas, except for the Christmas that I was sick. My mother wasn't told, she wasn't told that I was sent away to the TB hospital. She found out when my siblings went home for the summer. They never wrote to her or explained to her my sickness. My three youngest siblings were born while I was away. I knew about them because my mom would write to me now and then.

At Christmas and during the summer, it was really nice being home. A week or two before going back to The Mission I would shut down my emotions, my feelings. I didn't want to feel anything. I didn't talk about The Mission to my mom and dad. When we wrote letters home, they censored our letters. They would edit the letters and a lot of it was crossed out and we were given the letter back to rewrite.

Letter Writing and Sharing Emotions

My mother always wrote to us and her letters were censored coming in. She learned about writing what I call nonsensical letters, letters that didn't really have any feeling to them, just factual things. Even later on in life, my mom wrote letters where she would mention other people rather than write about the family. And she didn't answer the personal questions that I would ask her in my letters.

Our grade five teacher Mr. Point, as part of writing letters in English class, he knew about the letters we were allowed to write home, he gave us an example that we could follow:

"Dear mom and dad, just dropping you a line to say that all is well. I am fine, my brother is fine, my sisters are fine, we're all fine."

He knew the kind of letters that we had to send home. It's hard not to tell your experiences, and your parents never asked you about The Mission when you went home.

Effects

I remember talking with my mother, whenever it got emotional, when it was about sharing my feelings, my mother would shut down. I would see this veil would come in front of her eyes and she wasn't really listening to me anymore. I wasn't supposed to talk about feelings, so I learned to keep my feelings and thoughts to myself for the longest time.

My experiences made me determined to hang on to my culture, to hang on to who I was before I went to Residential School. It made me determined to know as much as I could about who I am as a Secwépemc person. I would argue with the nuns in my head, I would say, "No that isn't true, my people aren't a bunch of drunks, you don't know my people, you don't know my mom and dad, you don't know my granny." I would argue with them in my head. But I also learned to play their game. They wanted us to be good little Catholic girls. To be what we call Stemestut, 'white' on the inside. I learned to see the chapel as my place, the standing, the listening to the priest, which was all in Latin. I learned that I could automatically do all of that and my mind, my thoughts could be elsewhere. That was my escape, and it also gave me some breathing room because the nuns would think that I was a good little Catholic girl and they would keep off my back. In talking to some of the other girls years later, I found that many of the girls did the same thing. That they would go to church quite a bit and that was the reason for going, it was an escape. And getting the nuns to think that you were good little Catholic girls and not to push your buttons so much.

What all happened there, I believe it wasn't the church. I don't blame the church, I blame the individuals who abused us physically, mentally, emotionally, and spiritually, and I blame the government for allowing it to happen. I experienced all my life what that Indian Act was all about. Residential Schools are just one of those experiences.

I didn't want to hear the apology from the government in 2008. The ones that should apologize are the priests and the nuns. Sure, the government sent us there, but it was the priests and the nuns that hurt our people. I would have thought of it more if it were the Pope or the head of the Catholic Church in British Columbia apologizing. The government needed to apologize for more than the Residential Schools, like the Indian Act. I thought it was pretty empty myself.

I think it's important for individuals who went to Residential School to share their stories, so that it's not something just in your head, driving you crazy, keeping you down. So many of our people died because of Residential School, because of alcoholism the way they treated themselves because of Residential School, because they hated themselves, probably because they didn't think they were any good. Some of our people keep the legacy alive with the lateral violence in our communities, not just the members, but also the leadership and staff who continue their practice of 'lateral violence'.

The children and grandchildren, they need to understand what took place, and we need to look at how we raise our children and how we behave amongst each other because of Residential School. Like wanting to control, I guess that's a part of alcoholism as well, wanting to control. The Mission was all about 'power and control'. Almost every minute of every day was planned for you. You got up in the morning, you knelt, you prayed, you went to the bathroom, got washed up, you returned to your bed, you got dressed, went downstairs lined up, filed into the dining room, you prayed again. We would pray again before the meal and sit down and eat, then you would go do your chores. If you were grade three and up, you had chores to do before school. You would get in line single file, you would head out to the school block, go to your classroom, and before you sat down you would say a prayer. Everything was prayers and ritualistic. When you left Residential School, you carried that control into your daily life. The louder the nuns got trying to control you, the louder you got trying to control your family life. Try to control with fear, like they did at The Mission. Yell and scream and go berserk. We need to talk about the effects of Residential School. Behaviours only get touched on, some continue to make it an excuse, a scapegoat, but they need to change that behaviour for your family. A need to interfere, making other's business your business. It took me a long time to get out of needing control and wanting to change people. I came to realize that the only person I can change and that I can control, is myself. And I need to care about myself, to love myself, despite what I've been through, because of Residential School.

I went through an alcohol and drug treatment program and learned that a lot of my behaviour, from how I learned to react, was because of the Residential School. My mother also went to Residential School because our granny wanted her to get 'some schooling'. My dad never went to Residential School, he was supportive and left discipline up to my mother. And my mother, having gone to Residential School, would get mad at us about whatever and never talk about why we did what we did or said. There was no trying to understand what was going on, other than the anger. In the treatment program, I learned that I could change my own behaviour and the way I choose to react to others' behaviour. I learned that nobody made me mad, that I made the choice to be angry, to react with angry words. I slowly learned to care about myself, that I can be a loveable person despite what I heard over and over in Residential School.

My mother, having gone to Residential School, couldn't show us how she felt, or she could show us, but she couldn't tell us. She showed us how she felt by finding the right words in a card and giving us such beautiful cards. When I got a newer old car or reached my goals, my mom would give me a card so she could show us, but she could never say 'I love you, I'm proud of you'.

I learned to accept the different ways that she showed us. By picking berries, by working long and hard in her garden, by making Christmases awesome memories, by coming to visit us at Easter, so many ways she showed us that she cared and loved us. I don't remember others coming to visit at The Mission, but I could always count on my mom coming there at Easter. I had to learn to accept that my mother cared so much about us but she could never say it. She picked the cards that she gave us to say the words that she could never say. That's how I pick cards for my nieces and nephews, but I also learned to actually say what I want to say, to be able to say, with feeling and a smile, "I love you."

The friendships that we developed at the Residential School stayed with us for life. My mom talks about the friendships that were developed at The Mission, she called them her 'schoolmates'. I still have many of my friends from Residential School. I never would have met some of them if we had gone to school in our own communities. We knew the experiences that we went through together, knowing that we survived it, we didn't have to talk about it. I've lost a lot of friends over the years who were near and dear to me. Those that I don't see often, when we get together, we give each other a hug and catch up on each others' lives. My mom used to do that with her friends, they would start where they left off the last time they saw one another. That was something that the school couldn't have predicted, the strong friendships and the support we gave each other. We would talk about our hopes and dreams, what we would do with our lives after we left. If we wanted to, I'm sure we would have stronger unity amongst our First Nations today because of our common experiences, not only in Residential School but also 'living under the Indian Act'.

I had nightmares for the longest time after I left that place. I would remind myself in my dreams that the place was no longer there, that

I was no longer there, that there was no Mission. I tried keeping close to my two youngest sisters before I went away to high school in Prince George. In my younger sisters and youngest brother, I could see the loneliness, being lost, totally lonely and sad. I could see that feeling that I had when I started school, in my younger sisters. I talked to them when we became adults about that, about trying to spend time with them, reaching out to them the only way I knew how, we would just sit together. They weren't really talking to each other and after a while, they would be running around having fun. The first few months I would just sit with them, be with them.

A friend of mine asked me if I had gone to Residential School and I was floored because we were friends in Residential School. It showed me how traumatized some individuals were, that they chose to forget. Their mind chose to put some things aside so that it wasn't in their memory anymore.

At the Coqualeetza Sanatorium, we were cared for. There weren't so many rules to follow, the food was good, and the nurses and teaching staff were nice individuals. They didn't degrade us or degrade our parents. It was such a shock to go back to The Mission, there were so many rules, I was supposed to forget my 'Indianness'. What they didn't realize was that the more they tried to take something away from you, the tighter you held on to it. And during the summer, we were completely immersed in being Shuswap. My mom and dad took us out on the land where we hunted, fished, and picked berries. It was such a breath of fresh air to get back to that. To know who you are, to know that your parents were good, awesome people just by example. And not just our parents but our aunties and uncles.

My parents made sure that we knew why we went to the places that we went, to hunt, fish, and gather, that there was a history there. That it's been a part of who we are for the longest time, that the land is a part of who we are, and not everyone experienced that, which I think is sad. It's a question that keeps coming up in our community, "How can we take back our culture?" And my answer to that is, "Just live it." In saying that, it just made me realize how rich of a family upbringing I had, that my sisters and brothers had.

What my mother said when my sister and I went out to the powerline with her to pick wild strawberries, and my sister's little girl Vanessa was sitting on a blanket eating berries. My mom said, "I didn't think I would see the day when my grandchild would be eating berries." And we both just looked at my mom and said, "Did you really think that they would take that away from us at The Mission?" My mother was thinking that we would lose who we are by going to The Mission, not realizing that she and dad had always kept us living our culture and knowing and understanding the land. Now, one of my grandnieces has asked me to start taking her daughter out on the land. "It's time for her to learn the things that I learned from you," she said to me. We take the children out on the land and we also talk to them about it, why we are here, why we are picking strawberries, gathering juniper and swamp tea, and why we are fishing the trout in the springtime, because that's who we are. It's all part of who we are.

My mom taught us to think, not just to react but to think. I have always used my mind to keep me strong all these years. One thing I remember growing up was how the little ones, the 'papoose' as my mother called the babies, knew that they are loved. How people gravitate to the little ones when we get together. We hold them, and hug them, and talk to them before they are old enough to run off and play. The babies become the center of attention, a promise for a beautiful future. I learned from my mother, as my nieces and nephews came along, how our people look forward to the 'newcomer'. I came to understand that there is no such baby as an 'unwanted child', that we are all 'special and loved before we are born'.

"We were home for a couple of weeks at Christmas, except for the Christmas that I was sick. My mother wasn't told, she wasn't told that I was sent away to the TB hospital. She found out when my siblings went home for the summer. They never wrote to her or explained to her my sickness."

Jeremy Boston
(Phyllis Webstad's Son)

Jeremy Boston is Secwépemc, from Dog Creek/Canoe Creek.

I only went [to Residential School] for one season [in 1996], because it was considered a hockey school at the time. I went to Saskatechwan, it was Duck Lake Saskatchewan, St. Michael's was the school. I went there for a hockey school program; at the time, we didn't know it was a Residential School program. I went when I was 14 to 15-years-old.

I can't remember how we found out about this hockey school program there, but I had a choice to go, and I thought it was a great opportunity. I was doing great in hockey at that time when I was younger. I was one of the top goal scorers in the Kamloops Minor Hockey Association at the time.

First Day at School

My mom was always busy. She was always busy preparing for her future, I guess. Auntie Agness, she was a big part of our life, me and my mom, she kind of raised both of us. I remember the day I left for that school, my mom was working at Fisheries and Oceans at the time here in Kamloops, British Columbia, and I remember my auntie took me in her old Ford truck, we used to call the truck Bru. We travelled through Montana, all the way around back up to the border, and came back up to Saskatchewan. It was a memorable trip, to say the least. The hardest time was when my auntie left me there, and I was all by myself, and I didn't know anybody.

Photo of Jeremy Boston by Danielle Shack of DS Photography.

Day to Day Life

We lived in the dorms, you had to keep your bed neat and tidy every day. We were put in areas where we were closed off from the girls' side; there was a big cage. All the time we had together was only during school or eating time. It was kind of creepy, being a Residential School. We had limited supervision when we were there. We had nobody on our dorm floor, it was based on age category on each floor.

Being there was kind of hard at times because you have no family, you have no friends. The people kind of stay in their own province groups, because we're First Nations children from across Canada who went to that school. It was hard, there were people from Alberta stuck together, and I was the only B.C kid there, it was hard making friends. There was always the fear of fighting all of the time, and getting in each other's faces. It was a little clan going on with the provinces. Even though we played for the same hockey team, we still had rivalries between each other, just because we were different Nations. It was a fight for survival.

Impacts

The memories of going there, the first time leaving my own province, leaving British Colubmia, and my comfort zone. I will always remember some of the people that I went to school there with. There was this memory that sometimes it was fearful, and when I look back on it, it was because I was always alone; I always felt alone.

The Residential School System has impacted my grandmother — my moms mom, my Granny Rose, my mom, they all went to school. [It's a] big impact because we lost our culture for one. Me myself, I only know a limited amount of my own language. It was stripped away, starting from my great-grandmother Lena.

It was passed on from generation to generation, being pushed on to us being Christian, Catholic. I don't believe in all of that myself, I don't follow anything to do with churches myself. But I know that some of my family still do, but I just don't accept churches into my life.

Language is the biggest barrier that I wish that we could get back, we're never going to get it back. Language is gone in my opinion, all I have is a few words. I can't even teach my own children my language because we have no more teachers. The government did their job and took everything away from my family and all of the families that attended Residential School who lost their cultures, who lost their language.

Intergenerational Trauma

Growing up, my mom was 13-years-old, so I was raised by my auntie most of the time. There was a lot of alcoholism going on, and I remember bad relationships through my mother and my biological father. I still remember all of that. Breaking cycles is what I've been doing. I have all of my kids and my wife under my roof for the past 16 years.

My mom never experienced having a father around. My grandmother, I don't think they were a happy family all of the time. The father figure was just not there, and even in my life, I've never really had a father figure in my life.

Message to Students Learning About Residential School

The past is something that cannot be erased but can be healed through education and knowledge. Learn through stories; you're never alone, don't be afraid, your voice is powerful. Learn to forgive and move forward.

I will always remember some of the people that I went to school there with. There was this memory that sometimes it was fearful, and when I look back on it, it was because I was always alone; I always felt alone.

Mason and Blake Murphy (Phyllis Webstad's Grandchildren)

Mason Murphy, age 12, and Blake Murphy, age 17, are from Dog Creek/Canoe Creek. They are Secwépemc, Chilotin, and Chinese.

Mason and Blake are the sixth generation of Phyllis Webstad's family to be highlighted in this book, Beyond the Orange Shirt Story. The following are a few questions regarding Residential Schools that were posed to them, along with each of their responses.

Knowing that some of your family has attended Residential School, what do you know about the Residential School System?

Mason: What I know about the Residential School System is that the government would take kids away from their parents and take them to the Residential School. I also know that if the parents of the children refused to send their children that there was a threat that they may be sent to jail. Also, I know that the children, once they got to the Residential School, the children were stripped of their clothing and belongings and made to wear a uniform. In addition, I know the children would have to stay at the Residential School for 300 sleeps in a year. I know that children were prevented from running away to their home. Also, the children, I know, would not be allowed to speak their language.

Blake: It was messed up and they mentally abused kids, and physically abused them, causing life-time trauma.

Photo of Mason and Blake Murphy by Danielle Shack of DS Photography.

How do you think Residential School has impacted your family?

Mason: I think the Residential School impacted my family that we are not able to speak our language.

Blake: It made better and stronger people. But also a changed thought process of how beliefs have changed, such as culture, and loss of language. It changed to a white way — society, because of loss of culture and traditions.

Do you think it impacts you?

Mason: I think it has impacted me in that I am not able to speak my language. I think it has impacted me that I don't know all of my traditions.

Blake: I don't believe it has changed me, but it has impacted the current school system.

What would your message be to other Residential School Survivors and/or the children with parents/grandparents that went to Residential Schools?

Mason: My message to the people that went to the Residential School is never forget your traditions and culture. My message to the children with parents that went to Residential School is try to teach your children as much of the culture as you can.

Blake: I am thankful you survived to tell your stories, you are very strong and survived and are alive.

Are there any stories you have heard from family members that stood out to you?

Mason: My grandma's story.

Blake: What stood out for me was my grandma's story about Residential School.

What do you think is important for all students to know about Residential Schools?

Mason: I think it is important for all students to know to listen to Elders when they speak about the Residential School, to learn more about it.

Blake: That Residential Schools ethically messed up on what cultures could have been. Imagine what we could have been and what we could have learned if there were no Residential Schools.

Is there anything else you would like to share?

Mason: The only thing I want to share is that I like my school because I like English and Math and my teachers. I like school, I am able to socialize and go home after school to my family.

Blake: Please keep awareness of Orange Shirt Day. Continue to keep people educated. Allow schools to have visitors to share about Residential Schools.

"Mason: My message to the people that went to the Residential School is never forget your traditions and culture. My message to the children with parents that went to Residential School is try to teach your children as much of the culture as you can.

Blake: I am thankful you survived to tell your stories, you are very strong and survived and are alive."

Lynn Eberts
(Phyllis Webstad's Elementary
School Teacher)

Lynn Eberts is the kind teacher Phyllis Webstad had at the public school in Williams Lake that she attended during her year at St. Joseph's Mission Residential School. Lynn recalls her experience teaching students from the Residential School System.

I had...children [from the Residential School] for only one year, just long enough to have my heart broken. When we left that community, I didn't follow up on either the children or the Residential School System. I look back on those years, and my early teaching career, and wonder how I could have been so naïve.

In the late 1960's I was one of many eager, young, new teachers who knew little or nothing about First Nations culture or history when setting out on our first teaching assignments. We were very unaware and uninformed. We would see things on television or in newspapers showing First Nations people being so down and out. It struck some of us so hard and was incomprehensible. I remember thinking, 'Why don't you just go home?'

Having moved away, and being busy in our new community, it didn't cross my mind to explore the issues or situations I had left behind. We did, however, keep tabs on the abuse charges against the bishop. It made me sick to my stomach knowing what had happened in that Residential School setting. Those little children, their lives were in turmoil. As I later learned, people like Phyllis's grandmother had suffered terribly. They were deprived of their language, heritage, dignity, and the opportunity to learn how to parent. The ramifications of that have come up time and time again. Many First Nations adults still struggle to learn what was taken away.

When something comes up in the news or magazines about the past regarding Residential Schools, I am drawn to it because of my early teaching experiences. It wasn't just a British Columbia issue. Many parts of Canada had Residential Schools and there are many sad stories. Recently we heard about children dying from abuse or illness and being buried in unmarked graves with no record of where they were buried. That things like this happened is unthinkable because we pride ourselves on being decent people who expect other people to have the same level of decency.

There was a drive to Christianize and 'take the Native out of the Native.' The decision to do this went all the way up to the highest government and church officials who condoned it and believed that it was appropriate. There were many people in positions of power, in both government and the church, who regarded First Nations people as less than equal human beings and had no difficulty imposing their own values and language on them. Because First Nations people lived, dressed, spoke, and looked so different from the white majority, they were considered inferior and in need of being changed. It was a terrible mistake in the history of our country.

It was a very happy group of children in that primary classroom. We had a great year! In those days teachers were faced with far fewer social and behavioural problems in their classes. Children came to school with seemingly much less baggage. It was a very different atmosphere in schools back then, and although not all children came from happy households, they were much more respectful towards teachers. For me, it was a happy time, seemingly idyllic. I'm probably idealizing it a bit even though I am trying hard not to! I feel like an exceptionally blessed 'mother' to have spent time with all the little children! I have been a very fortunate teacher… There is a special bond you cherish in your role as a primary teacher, hoping that you positively impacted someone's life. I feel so glad to have been a part of so many childrens' lives...

I would like to have known and understood the ramifications of what was happening on the nearby reserve, in the Residential School, and in the community where I first taught. I did not know that it was a generational issue and that there was a history beyond these six-year-olds. I'm not sure that I would have felt confident or empowered to speak up or do anything, but I feel that knowing things would have given me another window into the childrens' lives beyond being their teacher. I wish I had known more about the children and their families as well. ...We know that there were some truly evil people involved who took advantage of the opportunity to be bullies and to hurt children. Many escaped notice or punishment because they were secretive. They lived in a relatively closed society where many other people were doing the same things and they didn't tell on each other. The children were so frightened...and who could they tell anyway?

That is part of the cycle of abuse. It's about thinking that it's happening to you because it's your fault. I am sure that some of these children were brainwashed into thinking that. We have to look at how the official business of changing First Nations people was condoned in many other countries around the world, the cultures that suffered and are still suffering.

Now it's the generational effect that we have to try and understand. Phyllis's Gran was in the system, and then her children, then their children after them. We didn't realize what we were taking away from them. How do you learn your history when your history was denied to you? How do you learn to be a parent when you have no role models? How do you learn your language? How do you share it when someone punished you for speaking it? It is incredibly lucky that there are Elders who are still able to teach the language and the culture, but they are not going to be here forever. We're losing them, losing them fast. Once you lose something or take it away, it is hard to get it back.

It is very sad when you see Aboriginal youth who don't have any connection to their culture. I think that the work Phyllis is doing, through sharing her orange shirt story, will help inform teachers, parents, and children about Residential Schools... Hopefully, her story will also give struggling Aboriginal youth a starting point for change in their own lives.

The trauma of being in a Residential School is very deep, and like a ripple on a lake after a stone is tossed, it ripples on and on, affecting even those family members who did not attend the school themselves. It is important to have a clear understanding of the history of what happened right near us because we are all connected in one way or another...

We owe a debt of gratitude to First Nations people because they taught newcomers survival skills; seasonal hazards, plant, fishing, and hunting knowledge. Unfortunately, they were repaid with smallpox, measles, alcohol, and abuse of children, women, and men.

There are so many First Nations people who still gather berries and herbs, and fish and hunt in ways taught to them by their Elders. I know some special people who routinely drive for hours to see their parents and grandparents and to share in these activities... I wish that there were more opportunities to take part in their culture, to know and to cherish what their parents and grandparents have taught them.

"The trauma of being in a Residential School is very deep, and like a ripple on a lake after a stone is tossed, it ripples on and on, affecting even those family members who did not attend the school themselves. It is important to have a clear understanding of the history of what happened near us because we are all connected in one way or another."

Photos of Phyllis Webstad's Family

Phyllis Webstad, age 6, at St. Joseph's Mission.
Photographer Unknown.

Phyllis Webstad, age 8, with the Dog Creek reserve
behind her.
Photo by Agness Jack.

Phyllis Webstad and Agness Jack displaying fish
caught at the Fraser River.
Photo by Vera Camille.

Phyllis Webstad, age 9, in Victoria, B.C. Her first time leaving the Dog Creek reserve since attending St. Joseph's Mission when she was 6.
Photo by Agness Jack.

Rose Wilson, Phyllis's mother, on the playground at St. Joseph's Mission.
Photographer Unknown.

Agness Jack, Phyllis's aunt.
Photo by Phyllis Webstad.

Helena (Lena) Jack, Phyllis's Gran, in her garden.
Photo by Vera Camille.

Great-grandmother Suzanne Edward Jim, outside the store in Dog
Creek.
Photo by Hilary Place

Gran Lena, 66-years-old, with Jeremy, 4-years-old.
Photo by Agness Jack.

Gran Lena with baby Jeremy Boston. The basket was made by Gran.
Photo by Phyllis Webstad.

Dog Creek Elementary School, the one room schoolhouse Phyllis
attended after her year at St. Joseph's Mission.
Photo by Louise Harry.

From left to right, Phyllis Webstad, Gran Lena Jack, and Jeremy Boston.
Photo by Agness Jack.

Top left to right: Jeremy Boston, Phyllis Webstad, Rose Wilson, Gran
(Lena) holding baby Blake Murphy. Five generations all together.
Photographer Unknown

Phyllis Webstad 21-years-old, with her dad John Butt (left) and her brother Buddy Butt (right) meeting for the first time this summer.
Photo by Jeremy Boston. 1988

Phyllis Webstad, age 14, and her son Jeremy Boston.
Photo by Agness Jack.

Phyllis Webstad, age 13, with her newborn son Jeremy.
Photo by Agness Jack.

Agness Jack and Jeremy Boston.
Photo by Phyllis Webstad.

Theresa Jack (back).
Front row, left to right, Phyllis's cousin Rose Jack, Lena Jack, Rose Wilson, and Phyllis with chewing gum. Dog's name is Toffee.
Photo by Agness Jack.

Left to right, Gran Lena, Gran's sister Felicia Harry, Vicky Tommy and Vicky's husband Moses.
Photo by Agness Jack.

Phyllis Webstad with her husband Shawn Webstad.
Photographer Shelley Webstad.

Phyllis Webstad in her Gran's kitchen as a little one, sleeping on her beloved tractor.
Photo by Agness Jack

Gran's house that was built on the Dog Creek reserve by the Department of Indian affairs in 1965. This is where Phyllis Webstad was born in 1967.
Photo by Agness Jack.

Barb Wycotte (left) with Phyllis Webstad (right) at St. Joseph's Mission.
Photographer Unknown.

Left to right: Elsie Murphy, Ron Murphy, Shawn Webstad, Phyllis Webstad, Hailey Murphy (little one in front of Phyllis), Jack Walker, Rose Wilson, Jeremy Boston, Dawn Murphy, Evie Murphy, Adam Murphy, Mason Murphy, Blake Murphy and Agness Jack.
Photo by Danielle Shack.

Phyllis (right) with her elementary school teacher Lynn Eberts at the book launch of *The Orange Shirt Story*.
Photo by Teddy Anderson.

Theresa Jack, 71-years-old, dip netting along the Fraser River. Behind her is a fish bowl constructed of rocks.
Photo by Sarah-Lee Philbrick.

Traditional style dip net used for fishing salmon. The original dip nets were made out of wood.
Photo by Sarah-Lee Philbrick.

Traditional Dip net being made by Phyllis's uncle, Raymond Jack.
Photo by Phyllis Webstad.

Salmon traditionally caught, cleaned, and hung on drying racks at
Phyllis Webstad family's fish camp along the Fraser River.
Photo by Sarah-Lee Philbrick.

A view of the Fraser River close to Dog Creek.
Photo by Angie Mindus.

Phyllis Webstad with her favourite flower, the yellow cactus flower, that grows wild on the Dog Creek reserve.
Photo by Shawn Webstad.

*"The cactus flower is a symbol of maternal love.
It can endure and thrive in harsh conditions and is therefore
symbolic of a mother's unconditional love.*

*In springtime, after the rains, the cactus flower is in full bloom on
the Dog Creek reserve and along the banks of the Fraser River. And
much like our ancestors who came before us, we will continue to
gather and prosper on our lands as we rise above the storm to
reclaim our way of life for generations to come.*

*We will continue to fish for salmon in the river, we will continue to
speak our language and practice our culture, and we will never
forget who we are. We remain resilient."*

~ Phyllis Webstad

St. Joseph's Mission Residential School

Residential Schools in Canada were a partnership between church missionary groups and the federal government. The government funded and regulated the schools while church missionaries operated them. Residential Schools were a major component of the Canadian government's efforts to assimilate Aboriginal people into the dominant white society. The goal was to force Aboriginal people to abandon their culture, spirituality, languages, ethical values, and traditional government and blend into the dominant white society. If successful, assimilation would have removed the government's legal and financial obligations to Aboriginal people as a group and given the colonists control of Aboriginal lands and resources.

The goal of the missionaries was to replace Aboriginal beliefs and practices with Christianity, European moral values, and a settled agricultural life. The missionaries pursued their work with fervor and little financial compensation because they considered it a sacred Christian duty. Both the churches and the government believed that Euro-Canadian culture was superior to that of the Aboriginal people, whom they considered "childlike" and unable to make proper decisions for themselves or their children.

Government and church groups both concluded, after other approaches failed, that assimilation could only be accomplished by isolating Aboriginal children from the influence of their parents at a young age and subjecting them to a rigorous European-style education for several years. The Canadian Residential School System was established to accomplish this, and the first Schools were built in 1883. Attendance was voluntary at first but the Indian Act was revised in 1894 to make attendance mandatory for all or most of the year. Non-attendance was punishable by parental fines or imprisonment.

St Joseph's Mission was started in 1867 by the Oblates of Mary Immaculate, a French Catholic missionary order who purchased land near Williams Lake, British Columbia. The location was selected partly because of its proximity to three Nations: Secwépemc (Shuswap), Tsilhqot'in (Chilcotin) and Dakelh (Carrier). After acquiring additional land by pre-emption and purchase, the Mission became a productive ranching operation, a base for missionary visits to surrounding Aboriginal communities, and the location of a day school for white and mixed race children.

The Mission day school struggled financially and, in 1891, it was replaced by a Residential School for Aboriginal children only. The School was supported by an annual federal grant, but funding was a constant issue and often inadequate to support quality education, care of children, or facility maintenance. The School was attended by children from the three nearby Nations as well as from the St'at'imc (Lillooet) Nation. Most students were Secwépemc. Only a few Tsilhqot'in attended prior to the 1930's. In the first year, eleven boys attended but, by 1950, the number was nearly 300. Prior to 1953, education included half days of instruction, primarily to prepare boys for agricultural work and girls for domestic work, and half days of industrial labour, with proceeds used to support the School financially. Year-round attendance was required in order for the Oblates to receive their full government grant. The curriculum was designed to prepare students only for low-paying manual labour and did not meet the academic standards of Schools for white children.

Teaching methods at the Mission required unquestioning obedience, strict discipline and speaking only in English. Transgressions resulted in harsh punishment. Hunger was common, food often poor, and sickness rampant in the poorly constructed buildings. The school attempted to destroy students' pride in their heritage, their family and themselves. The students suffered abuse of all kinds. The student death rate was high, and some who died were not returned to their parents. Dull uniforms were issued to prevent children from having pride in their clothing. Teaching methods and living conditions contrasted sharply with children's home experiences, and many students ran away.

In 1945, the school was declared an extreme fire risk and, in 1952, the dormitory for boys burned to the ground just after a new classroom building had been constructed. In 1964, the school was completely taken over by the Department of Indian Affairs, with the Oblates assuming new roles as counselors rather than teachers. By the mid 1970s, students were living at the Residential School, but most were bussed to public schools. The Residential School closed in 1981, and the facility was used briefly as Tribal Council offices and an adult training centre. Although the Secwépemc tried desperately to acquire the old school lands owned by the Oblates, the site was sold to a ranch in the late 1980s. The main building was torn down by the ranch over a period of years in the mid to late 1990s.

We would like to acknowledge Ordell Steen, Jean William and Rick Gilbert for their input, which allowed us to present this history to you.

Residential School Photos

A view inside St. Joseph's Mission Residential School bedroom quarters with the students performing their mandatory prayers.
Photo courtesy of Fonds Deschâtelets, Archives Deschâtelets-NDC.

Class photo from St. Joseph's Mission, also known as Cariboo Indian
Residential School. Rose Wilson, Phyllis Webstad's mother, is seated
in the front row 5th from the left. Year, approximately 1962.
Photographer Unknown.

Group photo from St. Joseph's Mission. It is believed Gran (Lena) is
present in this picture. It is believed that the photo was taken
between 1925 and 1935.
Photographer Unknown.

Photo of St. Joseph's Mission Residential School, taken in 1975.
Photo by Dave Abbott.

A view of St. Joseph's Mission Residential School campus and its students.
Photo courtesy of Fonds Deschâtelets, Archives Deschâtelets-NDC.

A view inside the chapel on the St. Joseph's Mission Residential School grounds.
Photo courtesy of Fonds Deschâtelets, Archives Deschâtelets-NDC.

Photo of St. Joseph's Mission Residential School after it closed in 1981.
Photo by John Dell.

More Orange Shirt Day Books

From Medicine Wheel Education

Author: Phyllis Webstad
Illustrator: Brock Nicol
Size: 8" x 7"
Pages: 24 pages +
Cover: Hardcover
Language: English
ISBN: 978-1-989122-24-2
$11.95

Author: Phyllis Webstad
Illustrator: Brock Nicol
Size: 8.5" x 11"
Pages: 44 pages +
Cover: Paperback
Language: English
ISBN: 978-0-9938694-9-5
$19.99

French:

L'histoire Du Chandail Orange

ISBN: 978-1-989122-00-6

Le Chandail Orange De Phyllis

ISBN: 978-1-989122-48-8